"*The Whole Man* is a tremend title suggests, addresses every with empowering teachings, equips men to face the challe and conviction."

—**Chris Broussard,** sports broadcaster; founder and president, The K.I.N.G. Movement

"*The Whole Man* embodies both a passion for the Black experience as well as a faithfulness to the Scriptures. It is invaluable in helping Black men navigate through the complexities of our journey in North America."

—**Dhati Lewis,** founder and president, MyBLVD; vision and multiplication pastor, Blueprint Church, Atlanta, GA

"Navigating the landscape of manhood is rough terrain for a Black man in America. We walk into so many meetings, schools, churches, and—far too often—relationships, feelings unseen and misunderstood. *The Whole Man* is a place to let our hair down and not only to be seen by other Black men but to allow the eyes of Christ to examine our hearts and souls. The writers of these reflections are dear brothers in Christ who've navigated this same terrain while still faithfully carrying the blood-stained banner of Christ. Allow these reflections to be a balm for your souls and a fresh touch as you continue to follow Jesus."

—**James Roberson,** pastor, Bridge Church, Brooklyn, NY

THE WHOLE MAN

40 SPIRITUAL REFLECTIONS FROM BLACK MEN ON THE HEAD, HEART, HANDS, AND SOUL

General Editors
RASOOL BERRY, DR. MALIEK BLADE, JEROME GAY JR.

*The Whole Man: 40 Spiritual Reflections from Black Men
on the Head, Heart, Hands, and Soul*
© 2024 by Our Daily Bread Publishing

Requests for permission to quote from this book should be directed to:
Permissions Department, Our Daily Bread Publishing, PO Box 3566, Grand
Rapids, MI 49501, or contact us by email at permissionsdept@odb.org.

Bible permissions statements can be found on page 155.

Interior design by Michael J. Williams

ISBN: 978-64070-314-8

Library of Congress Cataloging-in-Publication Data Available

Printed in the United States of America
24 25 26 27 28 29 30 31 / 8 7 6 5 4 3 2 1

Dedicated to the brothers.
We hope this forty-day journey contributes to the goal of
you being whole men.

Contents

Foreword

Over a decade ago, a string of manhood books was released. It was a bit of a renaissance when it came to Christian resources on issues concerning men. Many of those resources were geared toward a majority-culture demographic that was on the upper-middle-class side of things. Nothing is wrong with that at all. However, there were few that were from, to, and for people of color.

Someone may ask, "Why is there a need for resources for people of color?" Every culture and subculture has a voice. The truth doesn't change; however, the notes have to be in the genre that their heart is beating to. There are love songs in every genre of music: jazz, rock, country, R & B/soul, and hip-hop. But each one has different chords and tunes that connect with one's aesthetic. So it is with biblical truth.

The experiences of Black men are the same as our counterparts in so many ways, yet speaking generally, there are vast differences that need to be addressed by the gospel as contextualized to our experience. Contextualized to our families, work, education, experience in America, media, relationships with Black women, and focus and unique tenor as fathers in today's society. Even to our financial stewardship and wealth building.

Edited by Rasool Berry, Dr. Maliek Blade, and Jerome Gay Jr., *The Whole Man* is sure to set in motion a new movement of resources for men of color and men in general. In a day where there is resistance and confusion about manhood more than ever, there is a need to "be on the alert, stand firm in the faith, act like men, be strong" (1 Corinthians 16:13 NASB) Men all over the globe will spend time digesting this work for their souls in order to be better disciples, churchmen, servants, leaders, family members, and representatives of Jesus's glory in the world.

Dr. Eric Mason
Senior Pastor, Epiphany Fellowship Church

Introduction

A few years ago, ESPN released a film in their 30 for 30 series called *Broke* that sent shock waves through the country and became the source of debates from barbershops to coffee shops. *Broke* was inspired by a thoroughly researched *Sports Illustrated* article by Pablo Torre. He wrote: "By the time they have been retired for two years, 78% of former NFL players have gone bankrupt or are under financial stress because of joblessness or divorce. Within five years of retirement, an estimated 60% of former NBA players are broke."[1]

The film undermined the narrative that many Black men grew up hearing: making it to the pros as an athlete would grant you mental and physical health, wealth, happiness, perfect relationships, and a fulfilling life. Instead, the film showed that a host of former athletes who had "made it" were now emotionally, physically, and financially broke. If a majority of the men who reached the pinnacle end up broken, what does that mean about the state of most of us who never achieved that level?

Their stories uncovered a truth that had been silenced by shame. Despite challenging shifts in our culture that have shaken us, often many of us men suffer in silence rather than acknowledge and share our struggles about what it

11

means to go from brokenness to wholeness and from boyhood to manhood. But that has only led to more suffering.

Unfortunately, many men have few brothers to talk to. The Survey Center on American Life found that men in the United States who reported having no close friends went from 3 percent in 1990 to 15 percent in 2021.[2] Unprecedented millions of men have reportedly dropped out of the workforce. Some men find too much of their identity in the fear of being broke while others have lost hope of finding a meaningful vocation.

Men are disappearing not only from friendships and workplaces but from the church as well. "Despite being the largest ethnic group to attend a place of worship, 70–80% of Black men do not attend church services, either in-person or online."[3]

And tragically, our absence from these spaces of connection, hope, and purpose is having deadly consequences. "According to the Suicide Prevention Resource Center, young African American men commit suicide at more than three times the rate of African American women. The suicide rate for Black children ages 10 to 19 has risen 60% just over the past two decades, outpacing any other racial or ethnic group."[4]

However, regardless of the bleak reality these statistics reveal, all hope is not lost. In the midst of this dark crisis, there is light. To discover why we can look to a better future, we only need to look back to the lessons of the past. In previous seasons of despair, our ancestors found hope and guidance in the Scriptures and the Spirit. There we too can find the pathway to move from broken boys to whole men. The gospel of Mark records a man who was looking for solutions in a messed-up world. He too sought out a path forward, so he asked Jesus, "Of all the commandments, which is the most important?" (12:28). He wanted to know what to do. And Jesus gave him the way toward wholeness:

> Jesus answered him, "The first of all the commandments is: 'Hear, O Israel, the LORD our God, the LORD is one. And you shall love the LORD your God with all your heart, with all your soul, with all your mind, and with all your strength.'"
> (vv. 29–30 NKJV)

To be a whole man, Jesus taught, we must love God wholly. And He makes it clear in this passage that love isn't sentimental and soft but dynamic, detailed, and defined by action. Jesus identified four pieces of ourselves that when brought to God will make us whole.

Head: Our minds, thoughts, and the habits that contribute to our mental health

Heart: Our emotions, yearnings, and the principles that build healthy relationships

Hands: Our strength, vigor, and how we approach our work

Soul: Our spirits, struggles, and the source of our connection to God

Jesus proclaimed that this is the path to wholeness. *The Whole Man: 40 Spiritual Reflections from Black Men on the Head, Heart, Hands, and Soul* is designed to help you on the journey to being whole.

Read, reflect, and respond to the messages each day. But don't stop there. Watch the videos and discuss them with other men (find a discussion guide at experiencevoices.org/wholeman).

But don't stop there either. Let others know that they can be whole too.

This book is to help you love God through your relationships, mental and emotional health, work, and play, and with your soul. We pray you discover the richness of the Father's love for you. Regardless of where you might find aspects of yourself that are broken, we are here to help you heal and become the whole man you were created to be.

Let's get it in, brothers!

Rasool Berry, Dr. Maliek Blade, Jerome Gay Jr.
General Editors

experiencevoices.org/wholeman

HEAD
AND MIND

To set the mind on the flesh is death, but to
set the mind on the Spirit is life and peace.

Romans 8:6 ESV

We often weave the threads of faith, family, work, and community into the tapestry of life. The journey of Christian men is guided by the principles of love, compassion, and faith in a higher power. But amid these virtuous pursuits, there is one aspect of life that has been neglected for too long and has a profound effect on our well-being: mental health.

So we begin our journey to wholeness here, with an in-depth exploration of the importance of mental health for Christian men, revealing the essential connection between faith and emotional well-being. In our modern world, where expectations, responsibilities, and pressures increase every day, the importance of promoting mental wellness cannot be overstated.

As Christian men, we often find ourselves caught up in the delicate balance of providing for our families, serving our communities, and maintaining our spiritual lives. It is a noble pursuit, but it can sometimes lead to neglect of spiritual and emotional needs. In a domino effect, this neglect weakens our ability to fulfill our responsibilities with love, peace of mind, and perseverance.

In the following articles, brothers delve into the complex relationship between faith and the mind. We explore how embracing our spirituality can be a powerful source of strength and comfort, while acknowledging that sometimes even the most faithful among us struggle with emotional challenges. We discuss the stigma surrounding mental health in Christian communities and the urgent need to break down these barriers so that men, without fear or shame, can seek help and support when they need it. We encounter stories of Christian men who have weathered the storms of depression, anxiety, sorrow, and doubt and found hope and healing through their faith. Their experiences are lights that guide us to a place of understanding, acceptance, and compassion. We also explore practical strategies to promote mental wellness within our Christian faith, including prayer, meditation, community support, and professional counseling. These tools allow us to develop resilience, self-awareness, and emotional well-being while staying true to our faith.

We are embarking on a transformative journey that challenges us to redefine our understanding of strength and faith. We understand that emphasizing mental health is not a sign of weakness but of our humanity. By accepting this truth and weaving conversations about mental health into the fabric of our faith, we prepare to live a fuller, more authentic Christian life of compassion, purpose, and grace. It is our hope that, together, we will reveal to Christians the profound meaning of spiritual health and illuminate the path to wholeness in harmony with the teachings of Christ and the profound gift of grace.

Dr. Maliek Blade

 Scan to watch a conversation with men about loving God with our head and mind.

THE WHOLE MAN

IDK (I Don't Know)

We know that for those who love God all
things work together for good, for those
who are called according to his purpose.

Romans 8:28 ESV

IDK. We have all been in a space where life is hard and we
don't know why.

Dr. Charlie Dates, senior pastor of Salem Baptist Church
and Progressive Baptist Church in Chicago, once said, "As
for me, I'm learning to live with my questions until God is
pleased to give me answers." There are circumstances we
must endure and people we will meet that will leave us wondering why. For some personality types, having the answers
feels like a necessity just like water or air. Dr. Dates says
he is willing to wait for the answers, but many struggle to
get to that point or to accept that some answers may never
come. Those of us in this space must cling to the truth that
we have, as it is more real than the truth that we have yet
to find. This approach encourages us to focus on what we
know rather than what we don't know.

What do we know?

"We know that for those who love God all things work
together for good."

Whether the circumstances are positive or negative, in the
end they will be good for us in some way, shape, or form.
You may have a specific thing in mind that seemingly cannot

have any good result. Remember that the way it works for good may not be visible immediately. The way it works for good may not be understood easily. Reconciling the truth contained within Romans 8:28 can be difficult as we also seek to never make light of anyone's pain and suffering, including our own. The goal isn't to simply suggest looking at the bright side of things. The underlying truth that holds all of this together is that our Creator has good intentions for us. This is true no matter how it looks right now.

Remember the cross? Remember the death of Jesus Christ? In the moment, goodness seemed far off. But God was working things together for the good of His children even then. Brother, you as a believer in what Christ accomplished on the cross are a living example of the good that seemed only bad at the time.

We may have a level of insight about a given situation at any given time. But our view is limited. We must aim to trust the heart of God at all times. When doing so hurts deeply, we can take those grievances and questions to Him in prayer and know that He welcomes us.

Dr. Maliek Blade

What are some questions you struggle with not knowing the answers to?

How does the crucifixion offer hope that God can redeem "all things," even suffering?

How can the truth that God works all things for our good help us when we lack answers?

Psalm 56:8–13 ESV

You have kept count of my tossings;
  put my tears in your bottle.
Are they not in your book?
Then my enemies will turn back
  in the day when I call.
This I know, that God is for me.
In God, whose word I praise,
  in the LORD, whose word I praise,
in God I trust; I shall not be afraid.
What can man do to me?

I must perform my vows to you, O God;
  I will render thank offerings to you.
For you have delivered my soul from death,
  yes, my feet from falling,
that I may walk before God
  in the light of life.

Lost and Found

God is our refuge and strength,
a very present help in trouble.

Psalm 46:1 ESV

I was traveling with a group of friends, and I had one job: follow the taillights of a friend's SUV. But it was dark and I had absolutely no idea where I was going. As I paid closer attention to the vehicle in front of me, I realized I was following a stranger! I was lost on a back road in rural Mississippi, but I kept driving and didn't say anything to my friend in the passenger seat. A few miles later, I was still hoping I would find my way and see a familiar sight without anyone noticing.

Eventually, I turned to my friend, embarrassment emanating from my voice. "We're lost."

He replied matter-of-factly, "We can use the GPS."

This was back in the day, and I had never used a GPS before. My friend assured me the GPS knew where we were and could guide us to where we needed to be.

Without guidance, we get lost in anxiety, depression, and anger. The anger says, "Fight!" The anxiety shouts, "You will never get out of this!" The depression preaches, "You are here alone and nobody cares!" Their voices can be deafening, and the result is our veering off course. We get lost. Lostness is a state of confusion, stuckness, and stagnation.

As Black men, we are taught to keep driving in the lostness.

We have mastered the art of functioning while feeling lost. We wear carefully crafted masks that prevent others from seeing how lost we feel. We are experts at holding our tongues and not letting others know how we are plagued by lostness. We wander in the lostness, hoping we will find an exit. Yet the road seems to get longer and darker. The emotions get more intense, and before we know it we are off course and following a stranger.

Brother, take comfort that God knows exactly where you are and how to get you where you need to be. Though the anger, depression, or anxiety is intense, God has not left you alone in that state. He is a very present help in times of trouble (Psalm 46:1). He never has to run to you because He is already there. He watches over you 24-7-365. So wherever you find yourself, plant your feet and lift up your eyes, for God will be right there, ready to help you when you say, "I am lost." Follow Him because He will never lead you astray.

DeAron Washington

Are there any areas where you need to voice to God and others that you are lost?

What are ways you can prepare yourself for feeling lost in the future?

Psalm 121 ESV

I lift up my eyes to the hills.
   From where does my help come?
My help comes from the LORD,
   who made heaven and earth.

He will not let your foot be moved;
  he who keeps you will not slumber.
Behold, he who keeps Israel
  will neither slumber nor sleep.

The LORD is your keeper;
  the LORD is your shade on your right hand.
The sun shall not strike you by day,
  nor the moon by night.

The LORD will keep you from all evil;
  he will keep your life.
The LORD will keep
  your going out and your coming in
  from this time forth and forevermore.

DAY 3

The Interrogation

*Finally, brothers and sisters, whatever is
true, whatever is noble, whatever is right,
whatever is pure, whatever is lovely, whatever
is admirable—if anything is excellent or
praiseworthy—think about such things.*

Philippians 4:8

The year 2020 was supposed to be a time of abundant overflow for me. In hindsight, this was a self-proclaimed prophecy I boldly declared as a trauma response to heartbreaking disappointment in my career and personal life. I decided to move to LA in pursuit of my Hollywood dreams, I was in *Hamilton*, arguably the most influential piece of musical theater known to humankind, and my wife found out she was pregnant with our first child. All seemed to be trending in the right direction until a worldwide pandemic halted life as we knew it. Everything became a cloudy fog; misty melancholy took the Los Angeles skyline hostage. Depression began to swallow me whole like shark bait, and *lonesome* was an unexplainable melody I could not escape.

Suddenly I was stranded across country with no community or friends, the acting industry was decimated and my financial provision was vanishing along with it, and we had no support system or village to walk with us through the most important season of our lives when we were becoming new parents. I woke up every morning with extreme suicidal ideation. It's no secret that there has been a rise in anxiety, depression, and suicide in our culture, especially among Black men. No matter what I did to alleviate these feelings (prayer, Bible reading, therapy), nothing seemed to work.

There are three devastating lies the enemy implants into believers who are suffering from depression. God is absent, God does not care, and God will not intervene!

As all those thoughts took root in my mind, I asked myself an important question: Is this true? I pondered on the apostle Paul and his epistle to the Philippian church, and how he sat in a jail cell still praising God in the midst of his sufferings. That day I was inspired to begin a practice I called "the interrogation." It was a way to shift my focus to the Lord's goodness by putting my thoughts on trial in light of God's Word. If it wasn't true, if it wasn't noble, if it wasn't praiseworthy, righteous, lovely, pure, or holy, then it was a lie from the pits of hell trying to distract me from God's love.

This practice did not serve as a cure but merely a tool to fixate my eyes on the ultimate Healer. You see, depression is a multifaceted and nuanced mood disorder that has clinical and spiritual implications. But we have Christ, who felt all pain on the cross and still overcame the world. You will never be alone in your suffering because God's character reveals Him as the opposite of what depression tries to tell you.

Carvens Lissaint

Which of the three lies of the enemy is the most tempting for you to believe?

What thoughts do you have that need to be processed through "the interrogation"?

If you have thought about ending it all, or if you are in a season that seems too much to bear, meditate on the truth of Romans 8:38–39.

Romans 8:38–39

For I am convinced that neither death nor life, neither angels nor demons, neither the present nor the future, nor any powers, neither height nor depth, nor anything else in all creation, will be able to separate us from the love of God that is in Christ Jesus our Lord.

If you or someone you know is in crisis, call or text 988 to connect with the 988 Suicide & Crisis Lifeline.

Never Scared

The end of the matter; all has been heard.
Fear God and keep his commandments,
for this is the whole duty of man.

Ecclesiastes 12:13 ESV

It was 2003, and you couldn't step outside without hearing the hook to the single "Never Scared" from rapper Bone Crusher. It had recently released, and its perspective that men should never be afraid of anything went on to peak at number twenty-six on the *Billboard* Hot 100.

Whether a man goes to church or not, we tend to have a shared view of manhood and masculinity. This common view typically includes being tough, aggressive, or inflexible, and it most definitely includes never being scared. However, God commands us to fear Him out of reverence (Ecclesiastes 12:13). How do we reconcile these two perspectives? We cannot simply dismiss this requirement of fearing the Lord as a "newfound feminization" because Ecclesiastes was divinely written long ago.

God does not want, nor do our families need, men who are never scared. The better alternative is to direct our fear toward the right subject for the right purpose. The fear of the Lord in practice is not anxiety due to anticipated wrath from God. The fear of the Lord is obedience to God. We can humbly and confidently yield to God's leadership and obey His commands because of His character.

In many other instances, fear is seen as shrinking oneself due to the imposing nature of the opposition. While that can be a factor in fearing the Lord, there's more to the concept. When comparing the immortal God with mortal men, consider this: the fear of the Lord is a protective measure.

Brother, have you gotten yourself into trouble? Did your plan blow up in your face? Has the good thing you had in mind turned out to be bad? When we're able to set pride aside and acknowledge that we don't always know or do what's best for ourselves, we can then turn to God and bow before Him because of His spotless track record. So, don't discount or deny your fears; direct them to Him.

Dr. Maliek Blade

What are you struggling with being afraid of?

How can the reminder of Matthew 10:31 help you with that fear?

Matthew 10:28–31 ESV

And do not fear those who kill the body but cannot kill the soul. Rather fear him who can destroy both soul and body in hell. Are not two sparrows sold for a penny? And not one of them will fall to the ground apart from your Father. But even the hairs of your head are all numbered. Fear not, therefore; you are of more value than many sparrows.

I'm in Process

For I do not understand my own
actions. For I do not do what I want,
but I do the very thing I hate.

Romans 7:15 ESV

Our culture is obsessed with the outer man and outer woman. There are thousands of books, podcasts, online videos, articles, influencers, and even television shows that encourage you to change your outer self to achieve peace, tranquility, victory, self-discovery, and value. They'll tell you to lose weight, gain weight, or travel.

These are presented as the key to internal value, but they all fall short because the focus is external. External pleasure will never produce internal fulfillment! It's easy to see the issues everywhere around us but not the ones within us. We don't want to confront the enemy within, and we think that vulnerability makes us weak. But throughout the seventh chapter of Romans, Paul presents us with a different reality. He says the issue isn't something external, but rather it's internal: there's an inner battle we all face. We must embrace the reality that if we're in Christ, we're in process, and that process is called *sanctification*—meaning we're being conformed more and more into the image of Christ. Vulnerability and reliability with Christ are the only paths to sustainability.

Paul says, "When I want to do right, evil is there with

me" (see v. 19). He is speaking of the sinful capacity that lives in him still. If it were up to us, Paul is saying, we would do only what the law wants us to do. Yet we keep on doing the opposite. Paul doesn't mean that we do only evil or that we do more evil than good, but that the conflict with evil is one that keeps on.

The good news is that deliverance is possible because of the Deliverer. After sharing a struggle against our desires that we can all relate to daily, Paul doesn't leave us hopeless. He recognizes his inner war, but he knows that Jesus is the only one who can sustain him and give him victory over his desires. He's wretched, but he has a Savior who can handle his wretchedness.

You may struggle with things you hate, but the fact that you struggle and fight against desires that don't honor God is an indication that the Spirit is active in you! Keep fighting and know that God's power is your strength. In Him, you're not condemned; you're comforted, counseled, and compelled with purpose. Keep going!

Jerome Gay Jr.

Have you ever been there, finding yourself repenting of or falling victim to the same thing?

Are you real enough with yourself that you can admit your weaknesses? Explore whether or not you desire to practice obedience.

Romans 8:1–4 ESV

There is therefore now no condemnation for those who are in Christ Jesus. For the law of the Spirit of life has set you free in Christ Jesus from the law of sin and death. For God has done what the law, weakened by the flesh, could not do. By sending his own Son in the likeness of sinful flesh and for sin, he condemned sin in the flesh, in order that the righteous requirement of the law might be fulfilled in us, who walk not according to the flesh but according to the Spirit.

Not the White Man's Religion

May the peoples praise you, God;
may all the peoples praise you.

Psalm 67:3

"Christianity is the White man's religion!" This is something I often heard from my friends when I invited them to follow Christ. When I first heard it, I was dumbfounded and speechless because of my own experiences.

When I was in college, I took a trip to Ethiopia. During this time, we traveled to an island monastery established hundreds of years ago. Once our reed boats arrived on the shore of this island, we were given the opportunity to see the ancient Christian relics, like silver crosses and Bibles. Some of the Bibles in Ethiopia were so old that when you turned the pages, dust leaped into the air. They were proof of the Christian faith's ancient roots on African soil. I later learned of Coptic Christianity in Egypt and Nubian Christianity in what is now Sudan, and of churches planted in Syria, Iraq, and Iran way before the arrival of Islam. All these countries had worshipers of Christ, and they helped shape Christianity from its early years. So, I began questioning this narrative of Christianity being a White man's religion created to make slaves submit.

If Christianity was the White man's religion, then why did

it start in Palestine with Jews? How could it be that the church in Ethiopia is older than any of those in Europe? I also began to realize that if God did have a plan to save humankind, then it wouldn't be for just one culture; it would be for everybody. Jesus's name has been praised and the Bible has been translated in thousands of languages. It's not just the White man's religion. Jesus is for everybody, including me as an African American man.

Professor Lamin Sanneh once said, "Translation is the original language of religion in Christianity."[5] This means there's no one language or culture that owns Christianity. According to Philip Jenkins, by 2050 there will be an estimated three billion Christians, and only one-fifth of them will be White.[6] The vast majority will live in what is called the global South (Africa, the Caribbean, Latin America, and Asia). This seems like a new development, but it's actually a return to the roots of Christianity.

Saying Christianity is the White man's religion just doesn't add up. There are too many cultures in the world that have freely adopted Christianity from ancient times until now.

Ramon Mayo

What cultures have you seen embrace Christianity?

When someone says Christianity is a White man's religion, encourage them to look at the word of God in Psalm 96. Ask them if Christianity was intended for one ethnic group or for all ethnic groups.

Psalm 96:1–4

Sing to the LORD a new song;
   sing to the LORD, all the earth.

Sing to the LORD, praise his name;
  proclaim his salvation day after day.
Declare his glory among the nations,
  his marvelous deeds among all peoples.

For great is the LORD and most worthy of praise;
  he is to be feared above all gods.

Double-Consciousness

> If any of you lacks wisdom, let him ask
> God, who gives generously to all without
> reproach, and it will be given him. But let
> him ask in faith, with no doubting, for the
> one who doubts is like a wave of the sea
> that is driven and tossed by the wind. For
> that person must not suppose that he will
> receive anything from the Lord; he is a
> double-minded man, unstable in all his ways.
>
> James 1:5–8 ESV

We often see the words of James regarding double-mindedness used to illustrate those sitting on the spiritual fence. One foot in the world and one foot in the church. This double-mindedness is a challenge to our spiritual and cultural identities.

Over a hundred years ago in *The Souls of Black Folk*, W. E. B. Du Bois wrote, "It is a peculiar sensation, this double-consciousness, this sense of always looking at one's self through the eyes of others, of measuring one's soul by the tape of a world that looks on in amused contempt and pity."[7] Du Bois observed the double-consciousness that can sprout in us as society tries to devalue the culture of the minority group and inflate that of the majority. Du Bois wrote against this double-consciousness. James's position against it goes even further, as it impacts our spirituality. Doubting the goodness of how God made us would make us "unstable in all [our] ways." When we look at this Scripture from James, we see that it's rooted in a pursuit of godly wisdom that will stabilize us when doubt inevitably rises.

Being in the world but not of the world, and being Black in spaces that were not made for us, requires an identity rooted in Christ. The world will try to pull you back and forth and put you in a double-minded space. But your identity in Christ will anchor you. God has the final word, and He calls you His son.

Roy Dockery

How can you embrace the truth you know about your identity regardless of what you see in the world or how you feel? (See Psalm 139.)

How can you remind yourself that you are made in the image of God (Genesis 1:27) in spite of the images in the media or your environment?

Psalm 139:13–14 ESV

> For you formed my inward parts;
>   you knitted me together in my mother's womb.
> I praise you, for I am fearfully and wonderfully made.
> Wonderful are your works;
>   my soul knows it very well.

Bros

A friend loves at all times,
and a brother is born for adversity.

Proverbs 17:17 ESV

Some say "homeboys," some say "brothers," and others say "day ones." Not only do we have different terminology, but each of us may have vastly different things in mind when we consider brotherhood or friendship with other men. For some it's based on blood, and for others it's based on time spent together. We may be "bros" due to our common interests, or we may be friends because we started as work colleagues.

Each of us is free to define deep friendship differently. But Proverbs 17:17 singles out brothers and their role. It doesn't frame a brother as someone to simply shoot the breeze with but rather someone "born for adversity." Navigating through adversity together not only takes substantive communication but also helps build substantive communication by way of trust. Pivoting from shooting the breeze to substantive conversations with the bros may be awkward at first, but the "communication pyramid" can help get you started.

Here are some examples of the various levels at which we can share and become brothers in adversity. Substantive conversation occurs at levels 2 and 1, but many of us simply hang out at levels 5 and 4.

Level 5: "How are you?" Your brother says the cliché: "I'm good" or "Chillin."

Level 4: "Who won the Super Bowl in 2019?" Your brother: "The Patriots won."

Level 3: "The Patriots will have a hard time finding a suitable replacement for Tom Brady."

Level 2: "I bet on this game, and I'm worried I'll lose my money."

Level 1: "I have a gambling problem and need some help before it gets worse."

For some brothers, levels 2 and 1 come naturally. For other brothers, only levels 5 and 4 feel safe. Additionally, some of us are familiar with levels 2 and 1, but we only go there with the women in our lives, be it our mom, girlfriend, or spouse.

The goal is for you to find brothers you can express the fullness of your humanity to. Being more open in your conversation will put you in position to be that brother in a time of adversity and allow another brother to support you in that way without your pride or ego getting in the way.

Dr. Maliek Blade

Think of which brother or brothers you feel comfortable diving into levels 1 and 2 with. Schedule a time with that brother.

2 Peter 1:5–8 ESV

For this very reason, make every effort to supplement your faith with virtue, and virtue with knowledge, and knowledge with self-control, and self-control with steadfastness, and steadfastness with godliness, and godliness with brotherly affection, and brotherly affection with love. For if these qualities are yours and are increasing, they keep you from being ineffective or unfruitful in the knowledge of our Lord Jesus Christ.

Moment of Accountability

When a man's folly brings his way to ruin,
his heart rages against the LORD.

Proverbs 19:3 ESV

Pride and shame make it hard for us to accept fault when we actually are at fault. Rather than taking responsibility for our wrong actions or accepting the consequences, many of us resort to the following.

Gaslighting: Psychological manipulation where victims are purposefully and repeatedly given false information, which causes them to doubt what they believe to be true, including about themselves. In this case, a man's folly is manipulation.

Deflection: A defense mechanism that entails shifting responsibility for one's own error onto another person in an effort to protect one's self-image. In this case, a man's folly is lack of ownership.

Projection: Unintentionally attributing to someone else any undesirable feelings or characteristics that one doesn't like about oneself. In this case, a man's folly is attributed to someone else.

Avoidance coping: A dysfunctional form of coping in which a one modifies one's behavior to avoid contemplating, experiencing, or undertaking difficult things. In this case, a man's folly is evasion.

We may put the blame or attention on others or God when it should be on us. We often fail to see the ways we "blameshift" until someone who has suffered from it calls us out. Learning from our mistakes can be an opportunity for growth. Additionally, it will prevent us from hurting others with these forms of manipulation. These behaviors don't hurt only those we may consider our enemies. They cut even deeper when we use them on our loved ones.

Do you run when you hear about how you have hurt others? Have you mistaken accountability for someone throwing your past in your face? Keep this verse in mind: "Pride goes before destruction, and a haughty spirit before a fall" (Proverbs 16:18 ESV). Never accept responsibility for something you didn't do in order to quickly end the confrontation. That is a false sense of peace. However, when we are at fault, we should humbly accept it and attempt to make amends.

For men of God, the standard isn't perfection, but the expectation is for us to attempt to make right what is wrong. It is more honorable to own a fault than to hide it. Sometimes it's "them" at fault. Other times it isn't them. In these moments we can heed the words of the King of Pop, who challenged us to start our work with the man in the mirror and change our ways.

Dr. Maliek Blade

How comfortable are you with accepting accountability when you are wrong?

How might you improve or grow in this area?

James 1:22–25 ESV

But be doers of the word, and not hearers only, deceiving yourselves. For if anyone is a hearer of the word and not a doer, he is like a man who looks intently at his natural face in a mirror. For he looks at himself and goes away and at once forgets what he was like. But the one who looks into the perfect law, the law of liberty, and perseveres, being no hearer who forgets but a doer who acts, he will be blessed in his doing.

Brothers in Community

... not giving up meeting together,
as some are in the habit of doing,
but encouraging one another.

Hebrews 10:25

On a crisp fall morning, a group of guys gathered, seemingly for one purpose—free food! In truth, this event was a Saturday morning men's gathering hosted by a local church. The group that morning included several church members and their invited friends. But the group also included friends of friends, who had limited experience in church settings, as well as those who had negative past experiences with the church. All of this made for a potentially awkward Saturday morning interaction. Additionally, several attendees didn't know if this was simply a time to hang out or an event with preaching, or if it might even turn into a spontaneous prayer meeting.

Even with opportunities to join these types of gatherings, there are definitely times we'd rather be on our own, especially as we navigate the realities of existing as Black men in this world. But it's also essential that we engage in deep and authentic relationships with our brothers and even push through some of the reservations we might have. In today's Scripture passage from Hebrews, we're reminded to not neglect meeting together. While we all have personal preferences for relationship—whether that's hanging with a small group or large group, or simply interacting in one-on-one settings—we're called to meet together so we can encourage one another.

We all need to be encouraged. When it comes to our emotional wellness and mental health, this practice of community can impact our daily perspective and help us effectively navigate life together. On the contrary, as was highlighted by the COVID-19 pandemic, isolation and loneliness negatively affect both our physical and mental health. In following the guidance from Hebrews 10, we have an opportunity to support one another emotionally and in our overall health.

Looking back at that Saturday men's gathering, despite anyone's initial misgivings, what transpired was a time of rich conversation and fellowship. Throughout the morning, brothers shared honestly about their life experiences, joys, and challenges. Immediately after the gathering, some attendees spontaneously continued their conversation at a nearby coffee shop. It was a morning filled with laughter, authentic conversation, and deep connection. As a group, these brothers willingly engaged with one another. By taking time to pause together in community, they opened the door to new and deepened friendships, encouragement, support, and greater wholeness.

Dr. Nii Addy

Can you think of a brother or group of brothers you can intentionally connect with in the week ahead?

What does it look like to walk in authentic community with your brothers?

Proverbs 27:5–6, 9, 17

Better is open rebuke
  than hidden love.

Wounds from a friend can be trusted,
  but an enemy multiplies kisses. . . .

Perfume and incense bring joy to the heart,
  and the pleasantness of a friend
  springs from their heartfelt advice. . . .

As iron sharpens iron,
  so one person sharpens another.

HEART AND EMOTIONS

Above all else, guard your heart,
for everything you do flows from it.
Proverbs 4:23

We're often told the whats of Scripture but not necessarily the hows of Scripture.

- We're told to put on the whole armor of God (Ephesians 6:11), but we're not always told or shown how.
- We're told to go make disciples (Matthew 28:16–20), but we're not equipped with scriptural tools on how to share our faith with others.
- We're told to seek first the kingdom of God and His righteousness (Matthew 6:33), but not everyone knows how.
- We're told to cast our cares on God because He cares for us (1 Peter 5:7), but when it comes to grief and anxiety, we're not necessarily told how to release our cares.

As people of faith, we must be equipped with the hows, especially when it comes to being vulnerable and embracing our heartfelt emotions. Brother, this is important because grief will hit us all and we will need more than Christian clichés to hold on to. Studies consistently tell us that, worldwide, one in five of us experienced a mental-health struggle in the past week. So, we must know how to take care of and steward our emotions and allow ourselves to be vulnerable with others.

"We do not want you to be uninformed, brothers and sisters, concerning those who are asleep, so that you will not grieve like the rest, who have no hope" (1 Thessalonians 4:13 csb). Do you see the realness and hope in this verse? In comforting the Thessalonian believers that their brothers and sisters in Christ who had died would be raised again, Paul is essentially saying that while grief is real, when our hearts are rooted in Christ, we can stand and withstand the challenges that come our way. So, as you read this part of the book, I want you to think about how you would rate the condition of your heart currently—not physically but emotionally. Categorize the type of grief you may be dealing with right now, and then rest in the reality that this situation doesn't have to define you because Christ is the source of your identity.

Types of Grief

- *Disenfranchised grief*—when others don't consider your loss worthy of grief or signal that your grief isn't valid, so your grieving can feel especially isolating
- *Traumatic grief*—processing loss and trauma at the same time
- *Absent grief*—when you don't show signs, but you know it's there
- *Ambiguous grief*—loss of a dream such as a marriage, or loss that makes you feel incomplete

Identifying where you are helps you to move toward a healthy and rested heart. I want you to apply the four steps below and reflect on and replay them throughout your seasons of life to stay grounded and centered on Christ.

Four Steps to Grow from Grief to Gratitude

1. *Replay His rescue.* Recall the ways God has brought you through difficult situations in the past.
2. *Verbalize victory.* Speak it! Encourage yourself through your words and thoughts.

3. *Respect His timing.* Recognize that God's timing is not like yours.

4. *Sow your sorrow.* Reflect on the circumstances and situations that grieve you.

I want you to know that your soul care is essential to your health and stability as a man. Reflect on and replay these four steps, and let each devotion minister to your heart.

Jerome Gay Jr.

 Scan to watch a conversation with men about loving God with our heart and emotions.

Permission to Grieve

For everything there is a season, and a
time for every matter under heaven: . . .
a time to weep, and a time to laugh; a
time to mourn, and a time to dance.

Ecclesiastes 3:1, 4 ESV

If you've been on social media for a few years, you've probably seen the viral meme of the late rapper DMX breaking down in tears. What you may not know is the heartbreaking story behind it. In episode five of season one of VH1's hit show *Couples Therapy*, DMX opened up to his wife, Tashera Simmons, and host Dr. Jenn Mann about the severed relationship he had with his mother, whom he hadn't spoken to in eight years. With shakiness in his voice, DMX shared that he never got to call his mother or hear from her the words "I love you." Burdened by this sad reality, he broke down in tears.

What we see next is an abrupt turn in emotion that our culture pressures Black men to make. DMX wiped the tears from his eyes and launched into a speech of hardening and denial. "Man, I don't want to sound like a sucker," he said. "So what, she didn't say that she loves me? I'm here. I'm healthy. I got kids. I got a good career." Tragically, DMX, like many of us, felt that crying made him look weak. How many times have we as Black men asked ourselves that "So what?" question and rattled off a bunch of excuses as to why we shouldn't express pain?

In my own life, I've faced this temptation. My mom, my best friend, passed away surprisingly at the age of fifty-five on January 2, 2022. It was very tempting for me to harden my heart at the shock and confusion of losing someone so close to me, but instead I sat with the weight of grief and was eventually able to experience healing and peace.

God's Word offers us timely encouragement about grief. As Black men, we have permission to grieve and to reflect on what the brokenness of death, relational hurt, and unjust systems teaches us. There is a season and a time to weep and mourn (Ecclesiastes 3:1, 4). Jesus modeled this for us by weeping at the death of his friend Lazarus (John 11:35). Despite knowing Lazarus would come back to life, Jesus showed indignation at the evil of death and the enemy, which he later defeated through His death and resurrection.

James Seaton

Do you need to return to the pain you've dismissed in your life?

Read Ecclesiastes 7:1–4. How does the passage speak to you?

What are some reflections you can glean from the brokenness you've seen in your own life and in the lives of others?

Ecclesiastes 7:1–4

A good name is better than fine perfume,
    and the day of death better than the day of birth.
It is better to go to a house of mourning
    than to go to a house of feasting,

for death is the destiny of everyone;
    the living should take this to heart.
Frustration is better than laughter,
    because a sad face is good for the heart.
The heart of the wise is in the house of mourning,
    but the heart of fools is in the house of pleasure.

You Are Blessed and Forgiven

Blessed is the one
whose transgressions are forgiven,
whose sins are covered.

Psalm 32:1

Hey, my brother, how is your heart? Is it filled with unforgiveness as a result of resentment, comparison, grief, trauma, feeling unloved and unfulfilled?

The truth is, if you can relate to any of these emotions, you are not alone.

Picture this: You're in a room with brothers like you. They also want to trust and believe that they can let go of unforgiveness. Someone you trust is there to lead this accepting group. You sense God's gentle presence and invitation: "Blessed are they who are forgiven."

This is where permission starts—permission to put yourself in position to address any negative thoughts or cycles you have been repeating. This is where freedom starts, and freedom doesn't always mean a solution. Sometimes freedom is a release from the bondage we allow our thoughts to put us into. Unforgiveness is bondage. You deserve better. Holding on to guilt and shame distorts our identity as forgiven children of God. Unforgiveness insists we stay in the moment of our failure. Forgiveness is a constant choice to accept God's gracious word: we are more than our failure. As a result, forgiveness promotes the freedom to change how we see ourselves and what we fill our hearts with. Ironically, sometimes others forgive us, but we don't forgive ourselves. We even forgive others but not ourselves.

God's word over us is "Forgiven." Do we think our perspective or opinion holds more weight than God's standard? Sit with that for a second and ask the question, "How can we not offer ourselves the same grace that we give and that is given to us?"

You may be asking yourself, "What does forgiveness look like, and how do I practice it?" Forgiveness is when the mind makes a decision to no longer hold you hostage to your past, releasing your heart from its burden. Forgiveness does not mean forgetting; it means offering yourself another opportunity to show up differently. Forgiveness opens up space in the heart for love and freedom. Forgiveness attacks the lie that says, "You are your old self." Believe what Scripture says to you, brother: "Blessed is the one whose transgressions are forgiven, whose sins are covered." Here's a tip: keep reciting that verse when you're struggling to forgive yourself. Just like everything else, it takes practice at first. Give yourself grace for that too.

Take the pressure off your heart! You deserve it.

Paul B. Williams

In what ways do you struggle to believe you are forgiven?

What does 1 John 1:9 tell you about how to experience God's forgiveness?

1 John 1:5–10

This is the message we have heard from him and declare to you: God is light; in him there is no darkness at all. If we claim to have fellowship with him and yet walk in the darkness, we lie and do not live out the truth. But if we walk in the light, as he is in the light, we have fellowship with one another, and the blood of Jesus, his Son, purifies us from all sin.

If we claim to be without sin, we deceive ourselves and the truth is not in us. If we confess our sins, he is faithful and just and will forgive us our sins and purify us from all unrighteousness. If we claim we have not sinned, we make him out to be a liar and his word is not in us.

THE WHOLE MAN

A Pleased and Joyful Father!

The joy of the LORD is your strength.

Nehemiah 8:10

About forty years ago, an eleven-year-old boy played on a summer-league basketball team without scoring a single point in any of the games. Feeling defeated and crying his eyes out, the boy went to his father, who comforted him with a hug and told him, "Whether you score 0 or you score 60, I will love you no matter what."

From there, this boy had all the confidence he needed to fail because his sense of security and strength was in his father's pleasure and joy, not his own performance. He grew up to be one of the greatest basketball players of all time: Kobe Bryant.[8]

There's nothing a child wants—or needs—more than the sense of pleasure, joy, and love from their father. In fact, we're wired to learn the character of God—who He is, what He thinks about us, how He interacts with us, and why He interacts with us—through our relationship with our fathers.

Even though my dad was physically present and always provided for my family financially, he wasn't present emotionally, and I started believing God wasn't either. If you were raised by a stoic, distant, or emotionally absent father, you might see God in some negative ways or question whether He is pleased with you, is joyful over you, or even loves you.

If that's true, it's okay. Be comforted, because He's already told us all throughout Scripture so much about who He is (Exodus 34:6), what He thinks about us (Ephesians 2:10), how He interacts with us (Zephaniah 3:17), and why He interacts with us (Isaiah 30:18).

Similar to what Kobe Bryant's father told him as a child, but on a greater scale, God the Father said these words to Jesus before He ever performed a single miracle: "This is my Son, whom I love; with him I am well pleased" (Matthew 3:17). Since the Father is pleased with Christ, if you're in Christ, He's pleased with you as well. Rest your identity in the approval of the Father through Christ.

If you've given your life to Jesus, you don't have to wait for the Father's pleasure, joy, and love (Psalm 16:11). The joy of the Lord can be your strength right now!

Chaz Smith

What's one thing you have trouble believing about God's heart toward you?

What's one truth about Him you can remind yourself of to fight the lies and renew your mind?

Zephaniah 3:14–17

Sing, Daughter Zion;
   shout aloud, Israel!
Be glad and rejoice with all your heart,
   Daughter Jerusalem!
The LORD has taken away your punishment,
   he has turned back your enemy.

The LORD, the King of Israel, is with you;
   never again will you fear any harm.
On that day
   they will say to Jerusalem,
"Do not fear, Zion;
   do not let your hands hang limp.
The LORD your God is with you,
   the Mighty Warrior who saves.
He will take great delight in you;
   in his love he will no longer rebuke you,
   but will rejoice over you with singing."

What's Your Inspiration?

I have told you these things, so that
in me you may have peace. In this
world you will have trouble. But take
heart! I have overcome the world.

John 16:33

Jesus promised that life would be hard sometimes. We would be tired, troubled, and hurt. I have been tired when people have rejected me because of my skin color instead of trying to know me as a person. It was troubling when my teenage son was pulled over and accused of stealing a car I purchased for him. It was troubling when my wife felt unwelcome at a women's Bible study because of her assumed political beliefs. I was hurt to the point of rage when a college professor told me on the first day of class that I was taking a spot away from a qualified student. It was troubling when we were homeless twice. It was beyond troubling to have a doctor tell me I had cancer—twice.

These were all traumatic, trying, and tough situations, but they don't have to be defining. Christ understood suffering personally. He promised: "I will never leave you nor forsake you" (Hebrews 13:5 ESV). So now we can experience victory with the same Spirit that allowed Jesus to endure and overcome even death.

Jesus encouraged us to be inspired by Him when we are troubled. He gave us His Word to give us peace and a relationship with Him to inspire and empower us in these situations. He inspired me to forgive those people who wrongly judged me. He inspired me to work harder and have a dream when others expected so little of me. Because of Him, I could find things to be grateful for while going through cancer treatment. Because of His inspiration, I have learned to ignore how others may define me. Focusing on Him is a source of courage in a world that can truly break your heart.

Michael Lyles, MD

What or who is your source of inspiration to live a life that transcends a world full of troubles? Why?

Psalm 27:13–14 KJV

I had fainted, unless I had believed to see the goodness of the LORD in the land of the living.

Wait on the LORD: be of good courage, and he shall strengthen thine heart: wait, I say, on the LORD.

Spittin' Fire

Likewise, the tongue is a small part of the
body, but it makes great boasts. Consider what
a great forest is set on fire by a small spark.

James 3:5

On a summer day in 2016, four teenagers in Hamilton, Montana, walked away from a few hot embers burning beneath an extinguished campfire. They had no idea that a few hours later, the Roaring Lion wildfire would emerge from those tiny sparks, racing through 9,000 acres of land, consuming 14 homes at a cost of $11 million to suppress.

According to James 3:5, a single uncontrolled tongue can do the same thing in someone's life. Harsh words are like hot embers scattered around a dry forest. Just like those teenagers, we can easily toss around words and walk away, never realizing the immense devastation they cause long after they are spoken. We can attest to our own wounds from when someone cut us with careless words. Scientific studies have shown that overly harsh words can actually stifle proper brain function in children and adults, often instilling feelings of rejection, insecurity, inadequacy, anxiety, depression, humiliation, worthlessness, resentment, and despair.

A great forest is set on fire by a small spark!

But the Bible offers wisdom that can bring healing for those of us prone to use harsh words, as well as for those of us who have been injured by them. "Gracious words are a honeycomb, sweet to the soul and healing to the bones" (Proverbs 16:24). Jesus made himself known as gentle, compassionate, and approachable (Matthew 11:29), and we are most like our Lord when we follow this example.

For those of us who are not used to hearing or using encouraging words, it can be awkward to shift toward loving and positive speech patterns that reflect a more compassionate heart. But part of our Christian discipleship is taming our tongues to be generous with genuine encouragement. If you see something genuinely positive about someone or you appreciate something, offer a positive word about it. Be generous with encouragement. It's our job to build up others, not burn them down with our fiery words.

Where appropriate, incorporate some of these uplifting phrases into your conversations:

You are cared for and loved.

I will try to always be here when you need me.

I'm grateful for you.

You are so important to me.

Remember, Jesus said, "But the things that come out of a person's mouth come from the heart, and these defile them" (Matthew 15:18).

Mika Edmondson

When was the last time you shared a clear encouragement or compliment with someone else?

Who can you encourage with a positive word today?

1 Peter 3:9–11

Do not repay evil with evil or insult with insult. On the contrary, repay evil with blessing, because to this you were called so that you may inherit a blessing. For,

> "Whoever would love life
>   and see good days
> must keep their tongue from evil
>   and their lips from deceitful speech.
> They must turn from evil and do good;
>   they must seek peace and pursue it."

Trust and Submission: The Ultimate Follow-Through

Trust in the LORD with all your heart
and lean not on your own understanding;
in all your ways submit to him,
and he will make your paths straight.

Proverbs 3:5–6

Every golfer, including me, would like to be able to hit golf shots off the tee and straight down the middle of the fairway for three hundred yards like Tiger Woods. One of the reasons my golf game never experienced the three-hundred-yard drives that some of my golf partners did is because I would rarely follow all the way through the ball and trust my full swing. I would always wind up in the bushes, somewhere to the left or right of another beautiful fairway, looking for my golf ball just because I didn't trust and submit to my full swing.

Proverbs 3:5–6 reveals just how critical it is to "trust" and "submit" to the leanings of the Holy Spirit, who lives in each and every one of us who believes and confesses that Jesus is the Son of God (John 3:16). As a Black man who has lived for seventy-eight years in an unjust political and social system, the words "trust" and "submit" have become challenging to me. Repeated encounters with injustice gradually extract the idea of trusting or submitting to anything or anybody, making it a difficult proposition for day-to-day life.

However, the truth will set you free, and Jesus is indeed the truth (John 8:32; 14:6). I am trying to make better efforts to follow through with trusting God with all my heart in every situation, but now my follow-through has moved from my head and my mouth to my heart. To be a recipient of every blessing of God, I must take a full, prayerful swing for His promises. Trusting in our hearts and not just in our heads will always be a critical spiritual intersection for us Black men to experience the effectiveness of faith.

The green pastures and lush fairways of life that are God's promises to us are far better than the bushes of life that so many of us are experiencing every day because of our bad swings. Take a full swing and follow through with strong faith from your head to your heart. The promises of God are waiting.

Obie McKenzie

What are some areas where you need to follow through with your trust in God?

Psalm 62:5–8

Yes, my soul, find rest in God;
    my hope comes from him.
Truly he is my rock and my salvation;
    he is my fortress, I will not be shaken.
My salvation and my honor depend on God;
    he is my mighty rock, my refuge.
Trust in him at all times, you people;
    pour out your hearts to him,
      for God is our refuge.

Tough Guise

Frustration is better than laughter,
because a sad face is good for the heart.
Ecclesiastes 7:3

A colleague of mine, who has built his career as a therapist by counseling many troubled men, often says this to me: "Men wear more makeup than women do." He is not commenting on the recent trend of men placing substances on their faces to enhance their appearance. My colleague is pointing out how most men in Western society have been acculturated to avoid or cover up their most difficult emotions. The only feeling many men are comfortable with is anger. But even anger is more of a concealer than a revealer when it comes to manly emotions.

Makeup may be described as a cosmetic device, usually for women, designed to enhance one's appearance, hide imperfections, and change how one looks to others. By this metric, men use . . . lots of makeup! We just do so with our attitudes, speech, and behaviors, all of which can be used to misdirect ourselves and others from what we are really feeling. When depressed, confused, or anxious, men often externalize their angst through sex, bravado, violence, or even substance abuse. But what is it that we, as men, are so afraid of when it comes to our difficult emotions? Much like women, we seek to enhance our appearance, hide our imperfections, and change how others see us. These psychological and behavioral maneuvers can be traced to one leading cause: men fear inadequacy. This fear and the cultural pressure to hide it are at direct odds with whatever we are feeling. Men feel sadness. Men feel emotional pain. And men feel deep anxiety about many things.

But King Solomon offered an alternative to "manly makeup." He said that "frustration is better than laughter." And he asserted that a sad face is good for the heart. Solomon is teaching us as men that it's okay when our emotions get the best of us and become overwhelming. Solomon didn't view difficult emotions as flaws or imperfections that undermine our manhood. Instead, he saw anger, sadness, and depression as keys to our inner selves that need to be felt, embraced, and explored. Neither our manhood nor our faith is undermined by our emotions. On the contrary, difficult emotions enrich our faith, validate our manliness, and deepen our relationships with other men.

So, go to a mirror. Look at the man staring back at you. And give him permission to take off all of his makeup that's hiding who he really is.

Paul J. James

What steps can you take right now to be the man God designed you to be?

Could you benefit by getting professional help from a skilled counselor? If so, what do you think might be hindering you from seeking help (if you're not already)?

Who are the men you trust with your emotions? Will you reach out to them?

James 5:14–16

Is anyone among you sick? Let them call the elders of the church to pray over them and anoint them with oil in the name of the Lord. And the prayer offered in faith will make the sick person well; the Lord will raise them up. If they have sinned, they will be forgiven. Therefore confess your sins to each other and pray for each other so that you may be healed. The prayer of a righteous person is powerful and effective.

Dropping Bars

A brother offended is more unyielding
than a strong city,
and quarreling is like the bars of a castle.

Proverbs 18:19 ESV

I know a brother and sister who didn't speak to one another for nearly two years after a fallout over a game of
Spades. Although it seems pretty extreme, many of us can
relate to how relationship wounds can fester. When family
or friends hurt us, it cuts especially deep because the bonds
we share are so deep. In response, we tend to put up emotional bars around ourselves to ensure that we don't get
hurt again. Today's proverb is encouraging us to be patient
and persistent in difficult relationships. (Note: not danger-
ous and abusive relationships—difficult ones.)

There was once a prince who grew weary of living in his
Father's shadow. Despite the King's generosity to His son,
the young prince took His wealth and ran as far as he could
from the King. Over time the King sent His son a message:
"Son, please come home." The son wrote back, "I will not
and I cannot. I've spent all my wealth traveling to a far-off
land where you will never find me."

The King set out on a journey to find him. Sparing no
expense, after many years He finally found His son—poor,
miserable, sick, destitute, and alone. The son could not believe all his Father went through to reconcile with him. He

fell to his knees in tears. But his Father picked him up, embraced him, and took him home.

That's the love of God for us. The Father is pursuing you. The Bible is the story of how God would not allow our alienation to have the final say. He sent His Son and dropped the bars we built up to reach us. In Christ, God broke down the barriers of our guilt, sin, and everything that stood between us.

When we have fallen out with someone close, it takes real effort, energy, and time to make things right. Like a soldier seeking to enter a fortified city with strong gates, bars, and walls, we have to be persistent and strategic to wage peace. We cannot give up too quickly if we want to reconcile an estranged relationship. We need God's power to repent, to forgive, and to love—the power to say, "I'm sorry. I was wrong. I miss you and I love you."

It takes real power to drop the bars of resentment, stubbornness, and strife. Thanks be to God, we have that power in Christ.

Mika Edmondson

How can God's forgiveness help shape how you forgive others?

Ephesians 4:32 ESV

Be kind to one another, tenderhearted, forgiving one another, as God in Christ forgave you.

Colossians 3:13 ESV

. . . bearing with one another and, if one has a complaint against another, forgiving each other; as the Lord has forgiven you, so you also must forgive.

Man-to-Man Defense

Two are better than one.

Ecclesiastes 4:9

Few basketball fans argue the greatness of Golden State Warriors point guard Steph Curry as a shooter. Many even contend that he is the greatest shooter ever to play in the NBA. But Hall of Fame basketball legend Oscar Robertson, who played in a different, more defense-oriented era, offered some perspective about how the game has changed to allow for more open shots. "He's shot well because of what's going on in basketball today. . . . When I played years ago, if you shot a shot outside and hit it, the next time I'm going to be up on top of you."[9]

Notice that Robertson never critiqued Steph Curry's game. Instead, he pointed out the tactical deficiencies in today's NBA game. He pointed out that it's easier to score when you're not facing a vigorous defense.

Good character is the same way. When no one holds us accountable, our "game" may seem more polished than it is. Accountability is a biblical concept in stark contrast to our current cultural norms. Our world prizes privacy above almost all else. Families, schools, businesses, government, and even the church all play "zone defense." They only guard specific areas of our lives within their reach. But biblical accountability requires "man-to-man defense." The Scriptures put forth a prescription for 360-degree manhood that involves men cultivating deep investments in one another. The Bible describes all men as individual natural fibers. The only way we may achieve usefulness, significance, and enduring strength is to entwine ourselves in each other's lives. In this sense, a rope is a metaphor for manly accountability relationships. "A cord of three strands is not easily broken" (Ecclesiastes 4:12 CSB).

The alternative is that we live as single strands of thread, unable to bear the heavy realities of life in an ever-changing and uncertain world. We cannot measure our strength as men by our resilience as individual strands of thread. Instead, we increase our power when we decide to share our inner hurts, our life struggles, and our character weaknesses with other men.

Paul J. James

Have you cultivated a false persona that evades zone defense and avoids man-to-man defense?

Who has God placed in your orbit who can walk with you in accountability?

Ecclesiastes 4:9–12

Two are better than one,
    because they have a good return for their labor:
If either of them falls down,
    one can help the other up.
But pity anyone who falls
    and has no one to help them up.
Also, if two lie down together, they will keep warm.
    But how can one keep warm alone?
Though one may be overpowered,
    two can defend themselves.
A cord of three strands is not quickly broken.

Facing the New Normal

Therefore I will boast all the more
gladly about my weaknesses, so that
Christ's power may rest on me.

2 Corinthians 12:9

My left hand went rogue on February 10, 2021. I was banging out a memo on my laptop with the speed and agility of a Magic Johnson no-look pass, but as I rushed to complete my memo, my fingers stiffened, and something that just a minute earlier was as instinctual as breathing now required extraordinary effort. I consulted Google and breathed a sigh of relief, since it seemed like it was something minor.

Unfortunately, a visit to my primary care physician threw ice water on my self-diagnosis. Over the next few months, the doctors put all the puzzle pieces together and gave me the diagnosis I'd hoped against. It was Parkinson's disease, a degenerative disorder of the nervous system that disrupts connections between the brain and muscles.

I now had something in common with Michael J. Fox, former NBA star Brian Grant, the late Muhammad Ali, and nearly one million other Americans.

My initial response to my diagnosis was tears. Both my wife, Dana, and I held each other and cried out to God to guide and provide light for the scary and unfamiliar path before us. Our tears were a mixture of relief and sorrow.

Relief that we finally had an official answer, but sorrow for the sobering recognition that Parkinson's is a progressive disease that currently has no cure. I lamented the thought of gradually losing my independence and becoming a burden to my family.

Ultimately, though, I decided this "new normal" could be an opportunity for all of us to grow in our faith. In 2 Corinthians 12, the apostle Paul speaks about a supernatural experience of being swept into heaven, where he received revelations from God. To keep him from becoming too full of himself, God allowed Paul to be afflicted with some sort of physical ailment that was designed to keep him dependent on God's strength, not his own.

Don't get me wrong. My first choice would be to avoid a disease like Parkinson's, regardless of its faith lessons. Isn't there another way, Lord? But if in our broken and imperfect world God could use my "thorn in the flesh" (v. 7) as a platform for Christ's power to be experienced, then, Lord, let your grace prove sufficient (v. 9).

Edward Gilbreath

Reflect on ways that God redeems the brokenness of our world.

What are some new normals you've observed in your life?

Read Psalm 27:1–5. How does it speak to you? What can you learn from David about trusting God?

Psalm 27:1–5

The LORD is my light and my salvation—
whom shall I fear?

The LORD is the stronghold of my life—
    of whom shall I be afraid?

When the wicked advance against me
    to devour me,
it is my enemies and my foes
    who will stumble and fall.
Though an army besiege me,
    my heart will not fear;
though war break out against me,
    even then I will be confident.

One thing I ask from the LORD,
    this only do I seek:
that I may dwell in the house of the LORD
    all the days of my life,
to gaze on the beauty of the LORD
    and to seek him in his temple.
For in the day of trouble
    he will keep me safe in his dwelling;
he will hide me in the shelter of his sacred tent
    and set me high upon a rock.

HANDS
AND WORK

Let your work be shown to your servants,
and your glorious power to their children.
Let the favor of the Lord our God be upon us,
and establish the work of our hands upon us;
yes, establish the work of our hands!
Psalm 90:16–17 ESV

Moses had it all figured out. We read his credentials in Acts 7:22: "Moses was educated in all the wisdom of the Egyptians and was powerful in speech and action." You know you're a bad man when your skills are declared in the Bible! Raised as a prince in Egypt, he had studied under the nation's best and graduated from "Pharaoh U." Moses had a clear vision to help his people and a desire to lead them. But the problem arose when he tried to work it out his own way, and his passion turned to violence. In a moment, Moses caught a body and a case, experienced rejection from his people, and fled his hometown in disgrace. He became an anonymous man with an average life in the desert, shepherding someone else's sheep.

We can all relate to Moses in some way or another. Maybe the big dreams you once had when someone asked you as a child, "What do you want to be when you grow up?" have turned into bitter disappointment. Maybe the degree you thought would set you up for success has let you down. Maybe you feel like you're just shepherding someone else's sheep, helping them grow while you labor in obscurity.

Or maybe you achieved success but feel burnt-out, like it's all empty. That was Moses's story until he became a whole man. It all changed for Moses when one day, while at work, he encountered God in a burning bush. Experiencing God changed everything for Moses. He no longer defined his worth or evaluated his success based on himself but on God's revelation.

Moses would go on to meet with God for forty days on a mountaintop and eventually write, "In the beginning God created the heavens and the earth" (Genesis 1:1). Moses discovered something all men need to discover in order to realize our true identity: *we must understand God's purpose in work to understand our purpose in work*. Psalm 90 is the one psalm attributed to Moses. In it he prays: "Let your work be shown to your servants, and your glorious power to their children" (v. 16 ESV). Men, we are often misled in our culture to define our identity based on our work. It is no wonder so many of us find anxiety, despair, and disappointment in our jobs, and work so hard that we end up finding ourselves unhealthy—unable to maintain healthy friendships and relationships and even unhealthy in our bodies. Black men have the shortest life expectancies in the country. We are working ourselves to death. But there is a better way.

The devotions in this section help us get into the Word to reframe work from God's perspective. And not just work. The other thing we learn from Moses in Genesis is what God did on the seventh day: He rested. Dig into these articles to get into the true meaning of work and rest, and to experience what *The Whole Man* team is praying for you: "Establish the work of our hands upon us; yes, establish the work of our hands!" (v. 17 ESV).

Rasool Berry

 Scan to watch a conversation with men about loving God with our hands and work.

Work Was Good

In the beginning, God created the heavens
and the earth. The earth was without form
and void, and darkness was over the face
of the deep. And the Spirit of God was
hovering over the face of the waters.

Genesis 1:1–2 ESV

There is much to appreciate about the creation account in Genesis. We witness the preeminence of God, who has superiority over all things. We see God creating the world ex nihilo, meaning from nothing.

However, we can easily miss the simple observation of Yahweh (God) working and the related truth that humans are introduced as being made in the likeness of this working Creator. We also get the privilege to work.

The Architect of all that is good decided to offer us an opportunity to steward His creation. Although that original call faced a major setback in Genesis 3, the responsibility and privilege has not changed today.

How you work testifies to what you believe about God. If your posture toward work is self-seeking, then your picture of the Lord probably is too. If your posture toward work is that it doesn't matter, then your Lord is probably absent and negligent. However, if your posture toward work is charitable and innovative, then your Lord is likely to be generous and loving.

Work wasn't instituted simply to pass the time. Our Creator, Yahweh, did not innovate work out of boredom but in love. It was love that gave birth to work. We work to express our love and honor for a working God.

Our work is love because we work "as for the Lord and not for men." In Colossians 3:23 the apostle Paul writes, "Whatever you do, work heartily, as for the Lord and not for men" (ESV). Our work is not just about making a living or achieving personal success but about contributing to the good and flourishing of society and building God's kingdom on earth.

Let's be honest: despite its importance, work is not always fulfilling because we are faced with challenges and disappointments. We may struggle with burnout, boredom, and dissatisfaction. Oftentimes our work doesn't love us. We will encounter injustices, discrimination, or exploitation in the marketplace. But even amid these difficulties, we can find hope and redemption in our Lord and Savior Jesus Christ.

Here is the foreword to tomorrow's narrative. Will you treat your alarm clock as a reminder that today will present you with an opportunity to be fruitful and multiply goodness in a world in desperate need of it? Once you create out of love, will you rejoice and say that it was good?

Sho Baraka

How do you feel about your work?

How does thinking of your work "as for the Lord" impact your attitude about your work?

Ephesians 2:8–10 ESV

For by grace you have been saved through faith. And this is not your own doing; it is the gift of

God, not a result of works, so that no one may boast. For we are his workmanship, created in Christ Jesus for good works, which God prepared beforehand, that we should walk in them.

The Purpose of Work

The LORD God took the man and put him in the
Garden of Eden to work it and take care of it.

Genesis 2:15

It is interesting to observe how different days of the week
can affect our mood and attitude. Mondays are often met
with reluctancy and dread because it is the start of the work-
week. Fridays tend to be met with anticipation and excite-
ment because the weekend is approaching. It'd be nice if
every day at work was filled with anticipation and excite-
ment, but this is not the reality for most.

Many people are miserable at work because it simply serves
as a means to an end. As adults, we have responsibilities that
come in the form of bills. At times, our list of expenses can
become so overwhelming that we don't even keep track of
them. These expenses highlight the necessity of work.

Simply put, work is often viewed solely as a way to obtain money: we need to make money, and in order to make
money, we need to work. While there is nothing inherently
wrong with this reality, it can distort our sense of self. We
can end up defining our self-worth based on our net worth.
While wanting a high-paying job isn't wrong, the distortion
comes when our identity is exclusively tied to our job or
causes us to neglect other responsibilities.

Man did not earn, buy, or create the garden of Eden.
Instead, he inherited this paradise. As a result, he was to

maintain his inheritance. Maintaining the garden of Eden points to the concept of stewardship. The land and its resources do not belong to us but to our Creator. Therefore, work is about honoring God, who freely gave us the role of managing His creation.

Genesis 2:15 says man was to work and take care of the land. Though we are far removed from the agrarian culture of the Bible, these principles are very relevant for us today.

The purpose of work is not simply about obtaining money. Rather, it is about properly stewarding your current role or occupation. In doing so, you are acknowledging that God is the one who ultimately provides for you.

Brandon Russell

What are some things that frustrate you about your current job? What do you appreciate about it?

What would others say about the quality of your work? Can you honestly say you work unto the Lord and not man?

John 6:25–27

When they found him on the other side of the lake, they asked him, "Rabbi, when did you get here?"

Jesus answered, "Very truly I tell you, you are looking for me, not because you saw the signs I performed but because you ate the loaves and had your fill. Do not work for food that spoils, but for food that endures to eternal life, which the Son of Man will give you. For on him God the Father has placed his seal of approval."

Pieces of a Man

Yet when I surveyed all that my hands had done
and what I had toiled to achieve,
everything was meaningless, a chasing after the wind;
nothing was gained under the sun.

Ecclesiastes 2:11

In the song "Pieces of a Man," Gil Scott-Heron depicts a son discovering the burden of his father's shame. The father has become a broken man—symbolized by pieces of a letter scattered across the room—after being laid off from his job. The son is witnessing his model of strength and stability crumble, overcome first by helplessness and later rage. It's a melodic tragedy that's never too far from home.

The work we do to make a living plays such an important role in our feeling of self-worth. When a job is lost or our ambitions are dashed, we can lose hope and sink deep into despair. Many of us have always envisioned ourselves being the boss but end up under the management of others. We can feel like failures when our professional careers don't reach the heights we once expected.

Unfortunately, it's not uncommon to spend years regretting our decisions and lamenting how things turned out in our lives. We imagine how much better life would've been. Some in society judge us according to our résumé and material accumulation, and we can begin to believe those things would fill the void in our lives.

The Bible, however, directly contradicts the idea that fulfillment comes merely from career accomplishments and that our self-worth can be measured by the size of our salaries. In Ecclesiastes, Solomon explains that he attained many treasures, but he was emptily "chasing after the wind; nothing was gained."

Professional accomplishments aren't bad, but our fulfillment will never come from them. We're valuated differently in God's economy. He values faith, self-sacrifice, and service to our family, church, and community.

If you've been humbled by your career trajectory, don't "go to pieces." Our careers often aren't the primary way God uses us, and our humility makes us more useful to Him. A Little League coach, armor-bearer, accountability partner, or diligent Sunday school student and evangelist can be far more valuable to God than a *Fortune* 500 CEO. God is concerned with our spiritual state, and we derive our value from Him.

Justin Giboney

How do the Great Commission (Matthew 28:18–20) and Great Commandment (Matthew 22:36–40) contradict the idea that your worth is connected to your résumé and material accumulation?

Ecclesiastes 9:7–10

Go, eat your food with gladness, and drink your wine with a joyful heart, for God has already approved what you do. Always be clothed in white, and always anoint your head with oil. Enjoy life with your wife, whom you love, all the days of this meaningless life that God has given you under the sun—all your meaningless days. For this is your lot in life and in your toilsome labor under the sun. Whatever your hand finds to do, do it with all your might, for in the realm of the dead, where you are going, there is neither working nor planning nor knowledge nor wisdom.

What's in Your Hand?

Then the LORD said to him,
"What is that in your hand?"
"A staff," he replied.

Exodus 4:2

Over two million people were enslaved by the most powerful empire the world had ever seen. God heard the cries of His people and chose to intervene. But God's counter to Pharaoh and his legions of soldiers and advanced weaponry was an understandably overwhelmed shepherd. Moses was looking for a sheep who went astray, but God was looking for a leader who had gone astray because of failure.

We learn in Exodus 2 that Moses tried his hand at being an activist and failed epically. And as men, we can relate to the shame of failure Moses lived with, can't we? To protect ourselves from it, we'll run away from our calling and fail to recognize the opportunity God is putting before us. That's why God's interaction with Moses is so helpful. It reveals a key fact.

Your calling only requires that you use what you already have in hand. Moses assessed all the skills it would take to fulfill his calling and concluded he came up short. But God simply asked him, "What is that in your hand?" Moses answered, "A staff," probably wondering, *What can a staff do against an army? How can it get millions of people to listen to me?*

But God was showing Moses that his failures and his time as an unknown shepherd prepared him for this moment. God needed a man who could fearlessly confront predators of sheep and have compassion for those needing encouragement. A man who could correct and guide. And a man who knew he couldn't do any of it on his own. God had already prepared Moses through his trials and had given him all he needed to be a shepherd of Israel.

Moses, empowered by God, would later confront Pharaoh with his ability to turn a staff into a snake, water into blood, and a sea into a sidewalk.

Like Moses, you may have a calling or a desire for a career that seems unattainable. The key to your success is not your independence but your dependence on a God who can empower you beyond what you can imagine. You may be wondering how to bridge the gap between that dream that seems too big and yourself who seems too small. Look again, brother! God has already equipped you with what you need for this leg of the journey.

Rasool Berry

God will use whatever He has already given you to prepare you for the next step in the journey. How have losses in your past prevented you from trying to win in your present?

What's in your hand? What are the gifts, experiences, and abilities you currently have that can contribute to God's mission?

2 Peter 1:3–8

His divine power has given us everything we need
for a godly life through our knowledge of him

who called us by his own glory and goodness. Through these he has given us his very great and precious promises, so that through them you may participate in the divine nature, having escaped the corruption in the world caused by evil desires.

For this very reason, make every effort to add to your faith goodness; and to goodness, knowledge; and to knowledge, self-control; and to self-control, perseverance; and to perseverance, godliness; and to godliness, mutual affection; and to mutual affection, love. For if you possess these qualities in increasing measure, they will keep you from being ineffective and unproductive in your knowledge of our Lord Jesus Christ.

Liberated to Work

Commit your work to the LORD,
and your plans will be established.

Proverbs 16:3 ESV

On November 4, 1841, Frederick Douglass gave one of his first speeches, titled "The Church and Prejudice." In this powerful speech, given while still a fugitive slave, he had the courage to confront this global power's moral center—the American church—by sharing an unforgettable story:

> Another young lady fell into a trance. When she awoke, she declared she had been to heaven. . . . Her friends were all anxious to know what and whom she had seen there. . . . One good lady whose curiosity went beyond that of all the others . . . inquired of the girl that had the vision, if she saw any black folks in heaven? After some hesitation, the reply was, *"Oh, I didn't go into the kitchen!"*[10]

The mountain of racism was so colossal in the hearts of the people that its jagged peaks reached to heaven. In her mind (and the minds of many), Black folks belonged in the kitchen, invisible, banned from enjoying the fruits of heaven. This story reveals a dreaded insight into the psyche of the nation that unfortunately still lives today.

James Baldwin brilliantly pointed out that "history is not

the past. It is the present. We carry our history with us. We *are* our history."[11]

Are we aware of how this traumatic history has impacted us and contaminated our relationship with the vital activity we call work? In this nation, we as Black people were once deemed as property equal to a mule. We must deliberately shatter the oppressive psychological chains that attempt to attach our identity and worth to our performance.

Having once served as a career developer in my community, I've seen how heavy the reality of work, identity, and racial disparities weighs on people.

But I'm so grateful to our God that we are not unseen!

God does not need our labor but loves and desires us as sons. The King does not just send us to the fields but comes with us into the field and works with and through us for His good purpose (Philippians 2:13). There is a newfound freedom, peace, and fearlessness when we commit our work to the Lord, not man or unjust systems. Heavy burdens are lifted from our shoulders and anxiety around our performance decreases.

We can bring our full Black selves to our careers and workplaces in the light of Christ, living in His grace above obligation. In our commitment to Him, God anchors our plans, determining our future.

Donal Cogdell

Reflecting on Proverbs 16:3, what does freedom look like for you in your space of work?

Proverbs 16:1–4

To humans belong the plans of the heart,
  but from the LORD comes the proper answer of the
    tongue.

All a person's ways seem pure to them,
    but motives are weighed by the LORD.

Commit to the LORD whatever you do,
    and he will establish your plans.

The LORD works out everything to its proper end—
    even the wicked for a day of disaster.

A PSA:
The Proverbs 31 Leader
That God Requires

Speak up and judge fairly;
defend the rights of the poor and needy.

Proverbs 31:9

Countless articles, books, conferences, podcasts, and sermons have been devoted to the topic of leadership. Out of all the Scriptures that are referenced in understanding leadership, Proverbs 31 is often overlooked.

In the first nine verses of Proverbs 31, King Lemuel's mother imparts God's wisdom on leadership in what I call a PSA, or the principles of *prudence*, *sobriety*, and *advocacy*.

Prudence in Our Relationship Decisions
Is Vital to Our Leadership

Verse 3 charges, "Don't spend your energy on women or your efforts on those who destroy kings" (csb), and it underscores the fact that godly leaders avoid a decadent lifestyle that is categorized by unhealthy friendships and unhealthy romantic relationships. Picking people who are life-draining destroys you mentally, physically, and spiritually. Don't amass haphazard friendships or a harem of romantic interests. Find godly, life-giving friends and one wise and godly spouse.

Sobriety in Our Recreation and Self-Comfort Is Crucial to Our Leadership

Verses 4 and 5 point out that a godly leader avoids anything that will impair his judgment, because he realizes how important his judgment is for those who need it. When leaders engage in forms of self-comfort through abuse of alcohol or other substances, they are prone to "forget what is decreed, and pervert justice for all the oppressed" (CSB). In other words, godly leaders don't allow personal comfort to prevent them from leveraging their privilege for those who need help.

Advocacy, Mercy, and Justice Should Be at the Very Heart of Our Leadership

Verses 6 and 7 show that godly leaders rely on mercy to alleviate the suffering of those within their charge. Whenever people are suffering, a godly leader is empathetic and can ascertain what the people need. A godly leader empathizes by learning to "relive" the pain of others to help relieve their pain to whatever extent possible.

Verses 8 and 9 highlight that godly leaders speak for those whose voices go unheard. Kings and rulers during Lemuel's day functioned much like rulers of our day. They would plead the cause of elites, military leaders, aristocrats, and wealthy business professionals. Today, like then, elites don't need rulers to speak on their behalf. They have their own power, lobbyists, and lawyers.

When I was in business school, it was regularly pointed

out that the middle class is an accurate indicator of the health of a country. However, God says that the primary indicator by which He evaluates leaders is their advocacy for the poor, the needy, and the marginalized. Jesus called these "the least of these" (Matthew 25:40). They are the ones who have no voice in the corridors of power and who cannot afford to speak on their own behalf without the support of their ruler. Godly leaders speak for the powerless and the poor.

However leadership looks for you in your context, ensure that it reflects God's requirements of prudence, sobriety, and advocacy. Other people's flourishing depends on it.

Darryl Ford

Read Proverbs 31:1–9. What does prudence in your own relationships look like?

What does it mean for you to be sober-minded in your self-comfort?

What do mercy and justice look like as you advocate for others?

Proverbs 31:1–9 CSB

The words of King Lemuel,
a pronouncement that his mother taught him:

What should I say, my son?
What, son of my womb?
What, son of my vows?
Don't spend your energy on women
or your efforts on those who destroy kings.
It is not for kings, Lemuel,
it is not for kings to drink wine

or for rulers to desire beer.
Otherwise, he will drink,
forget what is decreed,
and pervert justice for all the oppressed.
Give beer to one who is dying
and wine to one whose life is bitter.
Let him drink so that he can forget his poverty
and remember his trouble no more.
Speak up for those who have no voice,
for the justice of all who are dispossessed.
Speak up, judge righteously,
and defend the cause of the oppressed and needy.

Perfect Timing

Of Issachar, men who had understanding
of the times, to know what Israel
ought to do, 200 chiefs, and all their
kinsmen under their command.

1 Chronicles 12:32 ESV

There are three timeless men who are and always will be imitated. They are athletes whose mastery of their sport causes them to be considered artists. The influence of Muhammad Ali, Bruce Lee, and LeBron James in our world has been and always will be timeless.

In 1967 at the height of the Vietnam War, Muhammad Ali was stripped of his titles because he would not fight in a war that he felt was unjust. He was sentenced to five years in prison. He endured ridicule and was even called a disgrace.

He avoided prison, but it was not until 1971 that he was allowed to fight again. In 1974 he used his "rope-a-dope strategy" with perfect timing to knock out the harder-hitting George Foreman to regain the heavyweight title of the world. He understood the strategy needed to win in the ring, and he understood the strategy needed to win politically and socially outside of the ring.

In 1972 there was another combat athlete who mastered his art with style and grace, who studied and copied the speed and footwork of Muhammad Ali. His name was Bruce Lee.

Bruce Lee also understood the times in a way that was timeless. His rejection of classical martial arts in favor of innovative new approaches was misunderstood by martial artists in the '60s and '70s. His last movie was made in 1973, and yet his philosophy on fighting is still referenced and imitated today. Could it be that Bruce Lee not only understood the times but knew his art would be timeless? His ideas have even influenced other sports stars who are not martial artists.

When interviewed several years ago, LeBron James suggested that he was motivated by Bruce Lee's ideas. King James quoted Bruce Lee when he said, "You ought not to be thinking of whether it ends in victory or defeat. Let nature take its course, and your tools will strike at the right moment."[12]

Not only did each of these men understand perfect timing, but they understood the times and they knew what to do.

First Chronicles 12:32 introduces us to a group of leaders who had the goal to make David king—to be a part of what God had designed amid the challenges of their time. King David had a temporary kingdom and was a preview of the King who rules and reigns today and forever, Jesus Christ. Considering that reality, may we embrace the leadership challenge of understanding the times and knowing what we should do.

James Alfred White

Who are your kinsmen who you can invite to strategize with you in understanding the times, considering the reality that Jesus Christ is our King?

1 Chronicles 12:38–40 ESV

All these, men of war, arrayed in battle order, came to Hebron with a whole heart to make David king over all Israel. Likewise, all the rest of Israel were of a single mind to make David king. And they were there with David for three days, eating and drinking, for their brothers had made preparation for them. And also their relatives, from as far as Issachar and Zebulun and Naphtali, came bringing food on donkeys and on camels and on mules and on oxen, abundant provisions of flour, cakes of figs, clusters of raisins, and wine and oil, oxen and sheep, for there was joy in Israel.

Rebuilding the City

"Please, Lord, let your ear be attentive to the
prayer of your servant and to that of your
servants who delight to revere your name.
Give your servant success today, and grant
him compassion in the presence of this man."
At the time, I was the king's cupbearer.

Nehemiah 1:11 csb

Nehemiah was enjoying the good life. As the cupbearer
to King Xerxes of Persia, he had regular access to the most
powerful man in the world. That meant he ate the best foods,
met with the most well-connected people, and lacked nothing. Nehemiah wasn't the man, but he was the man standing
next to the man. And yet, when he saw some fellow men
from his hometown of Jerusalem, he was compelled to ask,
"How is everything back home?"

What he heard was a horror story. Like many urban areas
today, Jerusalem suffered from dilapidated housing, danger-
ous streets, and a lack of infrastructure and leadership. The
city had faced attacks years before and never recovered. Jerusalem was down bad. Nehemiah wept and prayed. Though
his work was in the comfort of the king's palace, he never
forgot the plight of his people. What he did next reveals how
he saw his career as a calling. And how we can too.

Nehemiah prayed for God's guidance to use his position
to help fulfill God's agenda to restore. He then developed a

plan to use his access to the king to help those who lacked access but had needs. Then he proclaimed his request to the king. He asked for the resources to rebuild the city. He didn't rely on someone else to fix the problems; Nehemiah proposed himself as the solution. He volunteered to lead the building project and left the lavish palace to serve in the broken-down hood. Lastly, he learned from and listened to the people who were in the city before he offered a solution to their problems: "Let's rebuild the city!" Their enthusiastic response revealed the success of his plan. After various trials and tribulations, they rebuilt the city and their faith in God's faithfulness.

Whether we have proximity to presidents, principals, or princes, or we live in rough neighborhoods, God is looking for Nehemiahs who will pray, plan, and position themselves to use their platform to rebuild the city.

Rasool Berry

What are the broken places you see in your city?

How can you use your platform to rebuild the city?

Nehemiah 1:2–9

Hanani, one of my brothers, came from Judah with some other men, and I questioned them about the Jewish remnant that had survived the exile, and also about Jerusalem.

They said to me, "Those who survived the exile and are back in the province are in great trouble and disgrace. The wall of Jerusalem is broken down, and its gates have been burned with fire."

When I heard these things, I sat down and wept. For some days I mourned and fasted and prayed before the God of heaven. Then I said:

"Lord, the God of heaven, the great and awesome God, who keeps his covenant of love with those who love him and keep his commandments, let your ear be attentive and your eyes open to hear the prayer your servant is praying before you day and night for your servants, the people of Israel. I confess the sins we Israelites, including myself and my father's family, have committed against you. We have acted very wickedly toward you. We have not obeyed the commands, decrees and laws you gave your servant Moses.

"Remember the instruction you gave your servant Moses, saying, 'If you are unfaithful, I will scatter you among the nations, but if you return to me and obey my commands, then even if your exiled people are at the farthest horizon, I will gather them from there and bring them to the place I have chosen as a dwelling for my Name.'"

Bending Work for Greater Worship

Whatever you do, work heartily, as for the
Lord and not for men, knowing that from the
Lord you will receive the inheritance as your
reward. You are serving the Lord Christ.

Colossians 3:23–24 ESV

In my opinion, Denzel Washington is one of the greatest actors of all time, not just for his stellar ability to embody characters but for the ways he has committed his work to the glory of God.

According to *Christianity Today*, Washington says he "chooses roles that he can 'bend'" to preach positive messages through the film art form.[13] We can see this in *Training Day*, a movie where he won an Oscar for his portrayal of a corrupt cop. When Washington received the script for the movie, he wrote on it, "The wages of sin is death." He then recommended to the filmmakers that his character's ending be public and shameful to demonstrate punishment for his evil.

Some of us may feel like we don't have the luxury to bend our roles to "preach." In fields like investment banking, engineering, or marketing, we know we can't necessarily turn a stock or a client's social media post into a sermon. The good news is we can tailor our work to worship God no matter our field or responsibilities.

As a society, we tend to focus more on what we do versus how we do it. God is glorified through the latter as much as the former. God's Word calls us to "work heartily." In Colossians 3 and 4, Paul addresses conduct within Christian households and offers a relevant principle for all of us to apply. When he tells bond servants to "work heartily, as for the Lord and not for men," he is literally saying in the Greek to "work from the soul."

I grew up around Black women who cooked from the soul, mixing ingredients with love and giving special attention to each detail. Cooking wasn't always fun, as it involved standing over a hot stove and even washing dishes throughout the process, but the women around me still served with gladness. God calls us to do the same in our jobs: to serve with a smile, to complete projects with excellence, to care for our coworkers. We may not be doing what we're most passionate about, but that doesn't preclude us from moving with sacrificial love.

James Seaton

Do you need to adjust how you approach work?

Read Proverbs 14:23. How does it speak to you? How does this passage inform how you perform your day-to-day work?

Proverbs 14:20–23

The poor are shunned even by their neighbors,
but the rich have many friends.

It is a sin to despise one's neighbor,
  but blessed is the one who is kind to the needy.

Do not those who plot evil go astray?
  But those who plan what is good find love and
    faithfulness.

All hard work brings a profit,
  but mere talk leads only to poverty.

All Gas, No Brakes

Come to me, all you who are weary and
burdened, and I will give you rest.

Matthew 11:28

"Are you crazy?" These were the words of a student after asking me about my multiple roles. She approached me and asked, "What is it like being a husband, a father, a student, a counselor, and a supervisor?" Then she proceeded to question my sanity. It is at moments like this that I remember I am doing a lot. They remind me that I have Rick Ross syndrome, because "every day I'm hustlin'." I can easily slip into the get-rich-or-die-trying mentality. I have learned how to accomplish multiple tasks, but what I am currently learning is how to rest.

It is not abnormal in our time to have a nine-to-five along with DoorDash, Uber, or being a mystery shopper and a consultant. But have you learned to rest in our gig economy? Rest is tricky because we are rewarded for working without rest. You can get awards, degrees, promotions, and praise if you work without rest. Your bank account benefits from your toiling. Your labor is the way you put food on the table. However, what is the cost of living life with all gas and no brakes—or breaks?

We were not created to labor tirelessly without rest. God, who does not sleep nor slumber, modeled for us how to rest. In the act of creation, he worked six days and then rested. In Mark 2:27, Jesus stated that God instituted rest through the Sabbath because we need it. Working without rest is physically exhausting for us. It can cause our bodies to become dependent on caffeine and energy drinks just to function. Laboring with no breaks is emotionally exhausting for us. It prevents us from having the energy to be fully present with our wife, kids, friends, and family. Toiling tirelessly can be spiritually draining for us. It can result in us relying on our own strength and not trusting the care of our God.

Brother, are you weary and in need of rest? Jesus says He will give it to you if you come to Him (Matthew 11:28–30). God cares about your labor, and He offers you rest and refreshment.

DeAron Washington

What keeps you from resting? How can the knowledge of God's care help you rest?

Read Psalm 23 and meditate on God's care and offer of rest.

Psalm 23 ESV

The LORD is my shepherd; I shall not want.
　　He makes me lie down in green pastures.
He leads me beside still waters.
　　He restores my soul.
He leads me in paths of righteousness
　　for his name's sake.

Even though I walk through the valley of the shadow of
　　　　death,
　　I will fear no evil,
for you are with me;

your rod and your staff,
   they comfort me.

You prepare a table before me
   in the presence of my enemies;
you anoint my head with oil;
   my cup overflows.
Surely goodness and mercy shall follow me
   all the days of my life,
and I shall dwell in the house of the Lord
   forever.

SOUL AND SPIRIT

As the deer pants for streams of water,
so my soul pants for you, my God.
My soul thirsts for God, for the living God.
When can I go and meet with God?

Psalm 42:1–2

The Psalms are some of the most popular passages in the Bible because they speak to our souls. But what is the soul? Throughout Scripture, the soul is the life force in us that is able to commune with God but is also in touch with our minds and bodies. In Psalm 42, we read of the yearnings of our souls: "As the deer pants for streams of water, so my soul pants for you, my God."

Have you ever thirsted for a deeper connection with God? The second verse reveals you're in good company. "My soul thirsts for God, for the living God." The psalmist goes on to reflect on how unjust oppression and physical violence threaten him and cause a struggle deep within his soul. It's a struggle the Black community knows all too well, which is why *soul* is such a significant word to us.

"My tears have been my food day and night" (v. 3). Soul food originates from the story of the struggle to survive the transatlantic slave trade and being supplied meager food rations as enslaved people. But enslaved Africans transformed what was considered worthless and made it glorious. From the rice that Africans demonstrated the unique ingenuity to grow on American soil to the oxtails that were once deemed useless but now are regarded as a delicacy, soul food is a reflection of resilience in the struggle.

> These things I remember
> as I pour out my soul:
> how I used to go to the house of God
> under the protection of the Mighty One
> with shouts of joy and praise
> among the festive throng. (v. 4)

Soul music, with its dynamic blend of the lament of blues and the hope of gospel music, transformed music in America and became the soundtrack to the struggle. Tracks like "Inner City Blues (Make Me Wanna Holler)" by Marvin Gaye, "A Change Is Gonna Come" by Sam Cooke, and "Respect" by the Queen of Soul, Aretha Franklin, all were expressions of what it looks like to "pour out my soul." This tradition of honestly and passionately calling attention to the struggle is rooted deeply in the Christian tradition. Jesus himself sang soul music on the cross when he cried out, "My God, my God, why have you forsaken me?" (Matthew 27:46), quoting Psalm 22:1.

Rev. Martin Luther King Jr. picked up on this theme when he wrote of his approach to responding to the violent resistance to the Civil Rights Movement: "We will meet your physical force with soul force."

As you read this section on the soul, you will encounter reflections that acknowledge, "Brother, the struggle is real." Take them in with an open heart that's ready to resonate with the challenges of temptation, trauma, and doubt. Let these meditations guide you to see God's beauty more clearly, embrace His power more boldly, and receive His peace more consistently in your life in order for you to be a whole man. The struggle is real, but so is the God who gives "beauty for ashes" (Isaiah 61:3 KJV) and can revive your soul with hope.

> Why, my soul, are you downcast?
>> Why so disturbed within me?
> Put your hope in God,
>> for I will yet praise him,
>> my Savior and my God. (Psalm 42:11)

Rasool Berry

 Scan to watch a conversation with men about loving God with our soul and spirit.

Seeing His Beauty

One thing I ask from the LORD,
this only do I seek:
that I may dwell in the house of the LORD
all the days of my life,
to gaze on the beauty of the LORD
and to seek him in his temple.

Psalm 27:4

Beautiful is an adjective not often associated with men. Our culture tends to define beauty in ways that objectify women by emphasizing their appearance. While women are indeed beautiful, true beauty does not exclusively refer to how a person looks but who they are. This is why the psalmist seeks to gaze upon the beauty of the unseen Lord.

This subtle paradox teaches a profound truth. How can someone who is invisible be beautiful? How can the psalmist gaze upon the beauty of the Lord if he cannot see Him? The answer to these questions points to our purpose. We are designed to be in relationship with our Creator. Part of being in a relationship is getting to know the other person.

The psalmist appeals to this relationship with God in his time of distress. Though we may not be on the run from violent assailants like the author of this psalm, we will face difficult challenges throughout life. No one is immune to the trials of life. The question, then, is, How will we respond? If you live long enough, you will encounter moments of desperation, despair, and devastation.

These are the circumstances surrounding the psalmist. When we are in these desperate situations, we must fight the temptation to give up and let our anger fester. The psalmist is our example of how to respond to these situations. He knows enough about God that he goes to Him in his time of need. But if we appreciate the beauty of God's character, our relationship with Him won't just involve our needs in the moment but our trust in Him over time. If we know God is King, we ought to listen to Him. If we know God is sovereign, we should trust Him. And if we know God is good, we should gaze upon His beauty.

But what exactly does this mean? When we encounter moments of desperation, despair, and devastation, our attention is fixated upon these issues. When we constantly focus on these issues, we tend to fall deeper and deeper into hopelessness that can lead to depression and despair. However, there is someone more worthy of our attention and affection. The more we know about God, the more we should be fixated upon Him. This does not mean our trials and challenges will magically disappear. Rather, in gazing upon the beauty of the Lord, we are acknowledging that whatever the outcome, it is for our good and God's glory.

Brandon Russell

What are some things that have taken your gaze away from God?

What is something new you recently learned about God?

Psalm 27:4–6

One thing I ask from the LORD,
    this only do I seek:
that I may dwell in the house of the LORD
    all the days of my life,
to gaze on the beauty of the LORD
    and to seek him in his temple.
For in the day of trouble
    he will keep me safe in his dwelling;
he will hide me in the shelter of his sacred tent
    and set me high upon a rock.

Then my head will be exalted
    above the enemies who surround me;
at his sacred tent I will sacrifice with shouts of joy;
    I will sing and make music to the LORD.

Something Greater

You, dear children, are from God and have
overcome them, because the one who is in you
is greater than the one who is in the world.

1 John 4:4

One of my favorite shows to watch is *NCIS*. It's about Leroy Gibbs and his team of agents who investigate criminal cases for our country's armed forces. Due to the nature of their work, periodically Gibbs and his team will be on a submarine to solve a case. As I've watched *NCIS*, I've learned a lot about submarines. One interesting thing about them is that they are designed to go deep into the ocean. Ultimately, the deeper one goes underwater, the more pressure increases. This pressure can be so strong that it can crush you. Understanding this makes sense of submarines' unique, narrow, and compact designs.

A sub is designed to withstand the pressures of the sea, but for it to do so, there must be counterpressure on the inside. Submarines use built-in pumps and sensors so the external hydrostatic pressure is counterbalanced by the pressure within the submarine. As it goes deeper, the pumps change the internal atmosphere. In other words, there must be an equal or greater amount of pressure on the inside that counters the pressure of the outside!

In 1 John 4:4, John is writing to encourage us. He knows that in this fallen world, Christians will face temptations and deceptions. However, despite all of Satan's attempts, here is the good news: there is something stronger on the inside of us. God has not left us powerless. While the weight of sin desires to crush us, God gives us His Spirit that empowers us to push back on that pressure and achieve spiritual victory.

There is no temptation, no struggle, no pressure, no lie that the Spirit of God and His Word can't give you victory over. Despite the spiritual opposition we face, God has given us something stronger to withstand the enemy. The victory is ours. The victory is yours.

Be strong. Be courageous. Resist. Win.

George Moore

Read Luke 4:1–13. What do these verses tell you about Satan and temptation? What role does God's Word play in resisting temptation?

How can being filled with the Holy Spirit aid you when it comes to spiritual opposition?

Luke 4:1–13

Jesus, full of the Holy Spirit, left the Jordan and was led by the Spirit into the wilderness, where for forty days he was tempted by the devil. He ate nothing during those days, and at the end of them he was hungry.

The devil said to him, "If you are the Son of God, tell this stone to become bread."

Jesus answered, "It is written: 'Man shall not live on bread alone.'"

The devil led him up to a high place and showed him in an instant all the kingdoms of the world. And he said to him, "I will give you all their authority and splendor; it has been given to me, and I can give it to anyone I want to. If you worship me, it will all be yours."

Jesus answered, "It is written: 'Worship the Lord your God and serve him only.'"

The devil led him to Jerusalem and had him stand on the highest point of the temple. "If you are the Son of God," he said, "throw yourself down from here. For it is written:

"'He will command his angels concerning you
    to guard you carefully;
they will lift you up in their hands,
    so that you will not strike your foot against a stone.'"

Jesus answered, "It is said: 'Do not put the Lord your God to the test.'"

When the devil had finished all this tempting, he left him until an opportune time.

Wrestling with God

How long, LORD, must I call for help
and you do not listen
or cry out to you about violence
and you do not save?

Habakkuk 1:2 CSB

I grew up a wrestling fan. Wrestling was an integral part of my childhood, and I loved watching my favorite wrestlers like Ric Flair or Hulk Hogan get the crowd going crazy with their signature moves. The drama was something I looked forward to.

But my favorite wrestler was a Fijian-born man by the name of Jimmy "Superfly" Snuka. His signature move was to go on the top rope, and when his opponent was lying on the ground, he would jump off the rope, literally looking like he was flying, and devastatingly land on his opponent.

With that picture in mind, I now ask you: What do you do when you feel like God has done a Jimmy "Superfly" Snuka move on you?

You may feel like God has landed on you, smashing your hopes and dreams in the process. You may feel like Habakkuk, who felt crushed under the weight of life because of how God had chosen to move. You find yourself crying out like Habakkuk: "How long, Lord?"

I think everyone who has ever put their faith in God has

asked this two-word question, "How long?" It's a question about God's timing.

Habakkuk saw violence and injustice, and he cried out to God against it, but God didn't respond immediately. This led him to ask, "How long?" Many of us can relate. We've asked:

- Where was God during four hundred years of slavery?
- Where is God when unarmed Black men and women are being gunned down by police?
- Where is God when millions of unborn babies are aborted?
- Where is God when millions of teenagers are trafficked for sex?
- Where is God when there are millions of homeless people sleeping on the street?

These are all valid questions, but answers that blame the Creator for the actions of the creation make God the villain in human depravity. It's easy to blame God because we presume that since we can't see Him working, He's not doing anything.

We also get frustrated assuming that waiting for God to move means not moving at all. But sometimes waiting for God to move is the move! God's timing isn't about you getting older; it's about you growing deeper.

Waiting requires faith, the very thing required of the righteous (Habakkuk 2:4).

Remember these key truths about waiting:

- Waiting is active.
- Waiting strengthens your faith.

- Waiting helps you learn.
  - *Learn about God*—by spending meaningful time in His Word.
  - *Learn about yourself*—by taking this opportunity to become a student of your own heart as you're waiting and as your heart is revealed. Take this time to get a PhD in self-awareness.
  - *Learn about others*—by building meaningful relationships.

Jerome Gay Jr.

What are you wrestling with God about now?

How can the key truths above help you while you wait?

Habakkuk 1:1–4 CSB

The pronouncement that the prophet Habakkuk saw.

How long, LORD, must I call for help
and you do not listen
or cry out to you about violence
and you do not save?
Why do you force me to look at injustice?
Why do you tolerate wrongdoing?
Oppression and violence are right in front of me.
Strife is ongoing, and conflict escalates.
This is why the law is ineffective
and justice never emerges.
For the wicked restrict the righteous;
therefore, justice comes out perverted.

Cries of the Masculine Soul

I love the LORD, for he heard my voice;
he heard my cry for mercy.

Psalm 116:1

"Gangsta's Paradise," a song by the late rapper Coolio, is about a young brother who has spent his life in the streets. Gang activity, violence, and hopelessness are consistent themes you hear throughout his song. Some parts of the song that stand out to me in particular come at the beginning and the end of the first verse when he references walking "through the valley of the shadow of death" (inspired from Psalm 23). Coolio paints a compelling picture of realizing the futility of his gang activity and his own emptiness.

As I think about this song, I can't help but become overwhelmed with the emotion and nihilism described. Even if we've not struggled with the street life, how many times have we felt hopeless and wanted to cry out due to the pains of life?

Psalm 116:1 reminds us that God hears our cries. What I love about the words in this psalm, which is traditionally ascribed to David, is that he knew from experience that there is a God who sits high and looks low and that He cares about His children. David knew all too well what many men have faced:

- a father and siblings who didn't think much of him (1 Samuel 16:6–11; 17:1–29)
- a mentor who failed him (1 Samuel 18:5–16; 19:1–17)
- a giant who stood in the way of destiny (1 Samuel 17:40–51)
- a spouse who disrespected him (2 Samuel 6:20)
- enemies (both internal and external) surrounding him on every side (Psalms 3; 18)
- leading others while wrestling with his own fears (1 Samuel 22:1–5; Psalm 57)
- losing a best friend (1 Samuel 31)
- secret sin and scandals (2 Samuel 11:1–12:23)
- having wayward children and failing as a father (2 Samuel 13; 15:1–23)

Throughout it all, David trusted and knew that God heard him. He knew that God would answer him and that God would deliver him.

To my brothers who are struggling in their masculine soul, to my brothers who feel trapped and hopeless: God hears you. God loves you. God can deliver you.

George Moore

Read Psalm 116. How does it speak to you?

Who creates a safe space for you when you need to have tough conversations? How can they encourage you to rest in God's grace and compassion?

Psalm 116:1–7

I love the LORD, for he heard my voice;
   he heard my cry for mercy.
Because he turned his ear to me,
   I will call on him as long as I live.

The cords of death entangled me,
    the anguish of the grave came over me;
    I was overcome by distress and sorrow.
Then I called on the name of the LORD:
   "LORD, save me!"

The LORD is gracious and righteous;
   our God is full of compassion.
The LORD protects the unwary;
   when I was brought low, he saved me.

Return to your rest, my soul,
   for the LORD has been good to you.

Temptation

Watch and pray that you may not enter
into temptation. The spirit indeed is
willing, but the flesh is weak.

Matthew 26:41 ESV

I once asked my Uncle Kev how he managed to remain sober after decades of being mastered by narcotics. He looked at me and said, "I learned how to run." He didn't mean that he'd taken up the goal to complete a marathon. He simply meant that he learned how to escape temptation.

The Bible states in 1 Corinthians 10:13, "No temptation has overtaken you that is not common to man. God is faithful, and he will not let you be tempted beyond your ability, but with the temptation he will also provide the way of escape, that you may be able to endure it" (ESV). This text communicates that we all face temptations, we all have the spiritual resources to overcome them, and God will provide ways to escape them. The Scripture doesn't say God will give us a way to reason with temptation. We are told to escape it. So *we better learn how to run.*

Sometimes we have the tendency to try to negotiate with temptation, but temptation is savage and desires to consume all of us, which is why we must learn how to run!

Learning how to run is an ongoing exercise. One moment of temperance means nothing, because temptation returns with an insatiable appetite. Just like the act of physical running, learning how to run spiritually requires taking up some disciplines. Matthew 26:41 says, "Watch and pray that you may not enter into temptation. The spirit indeed is willing, but the flesh is weak" (ESV).

Be aware of the snares of the enemy and pray. Prayer is an acknowledgment of our weakness. We also need to get acquainted with confession. Confession isn't just about what happens after we fail to run. Confession of our weaknesses should occur before the tempting takes place.

When we confess our sins or our desire to sin, there is an opportunity for liberation. This is why Proverbs 28:13 states, "Whoever conceals his transgressions will not prosper, but he who confesses and forsakes them will obtain mercy" (ESV).

There was a season in my life when I tried to negotiate with temptation. I was too arrogant to run. But I was humbled and embarrassed by my actions. Praise be to God that it's never too late to confess our sins and learn how to run.

Sho Baraka

Will you confess your weakness? Will you pray for strength? Will you pick up those spiritual legs and flee the temptations that are chasing you down today?

1 Timothy 6:11–12 ESV

> But as for you, O man of God, flee these things. Pursue righteousness, godliness, faith, love, steadfastness, gentleness. Fight the good fight of the faith. Take hold of the eternal life to which you were called and about which you made the good confession in the presence of many witnesses.

Confessing in Community

Therefore confess your sins to each other
and pray for each other so that you may
be healed. The prayer of a righteous
person is powerful and effective.

James 5:16

I know spiders have a God-given purpose in the world,
but I never have liked them. My dislike for spiders was so-
lidified when, as a boy, I stumbled on a humongous web. It
seemed like it totally enveloped the upper half of my body.
I panicked and struggled to remove the sticky web from my
face. Suddenly, I felt something crawling on my neck. Intui-
tively, I knew it was the spider. I took off as if I were racing
Usain Bolt in the Olympic one-hundred-meter sprint! That
was a rough day.

Sadly, many Christian men, across racial and ethnic lines,
know what it's like to be trapped in the "web" of pornography use. Recent studies on this topic have noted that Christian men struggle with pornography as much as non-Christian
men. Such men have been caught up in the worldwide web of
lust, which repeatedly drives them to pornographic images.

By God's grace, I have experienced progressive victory
over lust and long-term sobriety from a porn addiction. This
would not have been possible without regularly engaging in

the spiritual discipline of confession. Confession to God is foundational, for when we fail to confess the sin of lust to Him, we will experience negative consequences. Psalm 32:3–4 says,

> When I kept silent,
>   my bones wasted away
>   through my groaning all day long.
> For day and night
>   your hand was heavy on me;
> my strength was sapped
>   as in the heat of summer.

However, confessing to God, as important as it is, is only half of the equation when it comes to biblical confession. James encouraged his readers to confess their sins within the community of faith (James 5:16). Every believing man must have at least one trustworthy brother (and preferably more than one) to whom he can confess sins of lust. Isolation is toxic.

When we engage in communal confession, we are supported by the body of Christ, who serve as the "hands" and "feet" of Jesus. Rigorous honesty in confession to one's brother fosters accountability. Mutual support and accountability are the keys to a life characterized by freedom and wholeness. My prayer is that you will be connected to a healing community.

This is a web you can disentangle yourself from. I'm living proof.

Joel A. Bowman Sr.

What temptations have you fighting to get out of a web? Have you confessed them to God?

What brother can you confess to in order to experience freedom?

Proverbs 28:13–14

Whoever conceals their sins does not prosper,
    but the one who confesses and renounces them finds
        mercy.

Blessed is the one who always trembles before God,
    but whoever hardens their heart falls into trouble.

The Natural Man versus the Spiritual Man

> But the natural man does not receive the things
> of the Spirit of God, for they are foolishness
> to him; nor can he know them, because
> they are spiritually discerned. But he who is
> spiritual judges all things, yet he himself is
> rightly judged by no one. For "who has known
> the mind of the LORD that he may instruct
> Him?" But we have the mind of Christ.
>
> 1 Corinthians 2:14–16 NKJV

When we look at Scripture, we see a contrast between two types of men: the spiritual man and the natural man. True spiritual manhood is achieved by pursuing and embracing the image of God, because we've been made in His image. But many men have a distorted view of manhood that is debased and appeals to our carnal desires. It's not manhood at all.

Meek Mill, one of the most popular hip-hop artists with MMG, had a song titled "I'm a Boss." In it he celebrates the money he's accumulated and the models he's attracted as signs of his manhood—even thanking God for them. His mentor and label head Rick Ross did a song called "The

Boss" that came out in 2008, with T-Pain singing the hook that points to much of the same. Many males are encouraged to obey their natural impulses to pop bottles and hook up with models, to be a boss, and to feel like a carnal king—but not godly men!

In pride we define ourselves by different distorted roles:

- *The Natural Man* defines himself by his sexual "conquests."
- *The Possessions Man* defines himself by what he has and owns.
- *The Fighter* defines himself by being tough and fighting, both verbally and physically.
- *The Life of the Party* defines himself by having fun and avoiding responsibility; he is undisciplined and depends on others to care for him.
- *The Busy Dude* never stops working. He's emotionally absent from the home, always on the laptop or cell phone.
- *The Comedian* laughs at everything and really isn't respected; his life is a joke because almost no one takes him seriously.

When we look at the Scriptures, especially the creation of man in Genesis 2, we see five components of the spiritual man of God:

1. A spiritual man is filled with the Spirit of God (v. 7).
2. A spiritual man's purpose is planted by God (v. 8).
3. A spiritual man is on mission from God (v. 15).

4. A spiritual man's actions are governed by God (vv. 16–17).

5. A spiritual man's appetites are submitted to God (vv. 18–25).

In spite of the fall, which awakened our flesh, we can still be spiritual men. God has given us the clearest picture of masculinity in response to the fall. He sent Jesus Christ, a man who took responsibility for what Adam destroyed. Today, because of Him, we can man up.

Jerome Gay Jr.

Jesus laid down His life. What do you need to lay down today?

Romans 8:5–9

> Those who live according to the flesh have their minds set on what the flesh desires; but those who live in accordance with the Spirit have their minds set on what the Spirit desires. The mind governed by the flesh is death, but the mind governed by the Spirit is life and peace. The mind governed by the flesh is hostile to God; it does not submit to God's law, nor can it do so. Those who are in the realm of the flesh cannot please God.
>
> You, however, are not in the realm of the flesh but are in the realm of the Spirit, if indeed the Spirit of God lives in you.

A Spectacular Move

But God chose the foolish things of the world
to shame the wise; God chose the weak
things of the world to shame the strong.

1 Corinthians 1:27

It's a moment in time that most who witnessed it will never forget. In game two of the 1991 NBA Finals, the Chicago Bulls, led by "His Airness," Michael Jordan, did the unthinkable. Jordan, seemingly en route to scoring on a right-hand layup, unexpectedly switched the ball to his left hand and perfectly kissed it off the backboard for arguably one of the most athletic, acrobatic basketball scoring moves since Dr. J's famous reverse layup behind the basket. Marv Albert was the broadcast commentator, and he emphatically bellowed, "A spectacular move by Michael Jordan!"

But why was Jordan's switching to his left hand and making the shot so memorable? Answer: because it put on full display his unmatched skill, which defied logic and led his teams to victory all six times they appeared in the championship series.

We are awed by witnessing the glory of power, wisdom, and skill that defy perceived limitations and bring about victory. And that's one of the attractions of what Jesus Christ accomplished in His own life. In 1 Corinthians 1:27, we read of the impressive move the only One rightfully considered the greatest of all time (GOAT) performed via the cross—a feat that still causes us to marvel today. He died so we could have life. He defeated death through the resurrection. He chose the foolish things to shame the wise, the weak things to shame the strong, and all of this to bring us into a loving, living, lasting union with Him. And the good news is that He's not done yet! Jesus promises to bring forth victory in your life. There's a spectacular move by our undefeated, mighty God with your name on it, so please don't lose heart!

Chuck Reed

In what areas of your life are you relying on your strength and wisdom and not on the Lord's strength and wisdom?

1 Corinthians 1:26–31

Brothers and sisters, think of what you were when you were called. Not many of you were wise by human standards; not many were influential; not many were of noble birth. But God chose the foolish things of the world to shame the wise; God chose the weak things of the world to shame the strong. God chose the lowly things of this world and the despised things—and the things that are not—to nullify the things that are, so that no one may boast before him. It is because of him that you are in Christ Jesus, who has become for us wisdom from God—that is, our righteousness, holiness and redemption. Therefore, as it is written: "Let the one who boasts boast in the Lord."

Greater Expectations

Then he touched their eyes and said,
"According to your faith let it be done to you."
Matthew 9:29

What if I were to tell you that without even knowing you, I
know exactly what God is doing in your life right now? The
answer: exactly what you expect Him to.

Am I implying that you can control God? No. But according to Jesus, we experience exactly what we expect
from Him.

In Matthew 9:28, Jesus asked two blind men who were
seeking healing: "Do you believe that I am able to do this?"

"Yes, Lord," they replied.

Notice that it's only after they affirm their belief in what
Jesus could do in them that Jesus says, "According to your
faith let it be done to you." The point of faith is not believing God for whatever we want but believing that He will be
who He says He is. If we can believe God to be God, then
our expectations of Him should not fade over time but rather
increase. But this is not the case for so many men who follow Jesus because disappointment happens in our lives and
leads to what I call decreased expectations. For instance, you
get saved and have this zeal for Jesus you can't wait to tell
people about, but eventually the euphoria of that moment
fades. You begin to experience disappointments. You witness
hypocrisy in people you trust, lose a close friend, or meet a

tragedy. Over time these disappointments lead to decreased expectations. You no longer know how to answer the question: *Do I believe that Jesus is able do this?*

But God has so much more for you. The reality on this side of heaven is that you and I must live with what one author calls *ambidextrous faith*: a faith that simultaneously holds God's blessings in our right hand and difficulty in our left.[14]

When we experience hardship, we can become prisoners of decreased expectations of God. But God never leaves nor abandons us, and even when He disciplines us, He loves us.

Brother, no matter how rough life has been and how low you've fallen, God can still use you! Instead of giving up, hold on to greater expectations. The line that separates superficial faith from substantial faith is our expectations.

Expect God to do great things in you, through you, and around you.

Jerome Gay Jr.

Do you believe God is able to do this? Why or why not?

Recall a time when you had great expectations of God. What has caused those expectations to increase or decrease over time?

Ephesians 3:20–21

Now to him who is able to do immeasurably more than all we ask or imagine, according to his power that is at work within us, to him be glory in the church and in Christ Jesus throughout all generations, for ever and ever! Amen.

Peace Out!

The LORD bless you
and keep you;
the LORD make his face shine on you
and be gracious to you;
the LORD turn his face toward you
and give you peace.

Numbers 6:24–26

When I was a boy, "Peace!" was exclaimed constantly in popular culture. Petitions for peace ranged from "Peace in the Middle East!" to the final lyrics of the latest hip-hop song. Celebrities adorning the pages of my favorite magazines or the posters on my bedroom wall often posed with two fingers lifted in the air, the universal sign for peace.

The peace lauded in my youth was primarily a call to end violence in our communities and war abroad. When most people think of peace, it is the end of physical violence or a state of tranquility that immediately comes to mind. Certainly these notions of peace are things we should continue to pursue. Yet, there is another form of peace to which we should also aspire.

In Numbers, the Lord tells Moses to share a blessing with Aaron, the high priest, who is then to share this blessing with the people of Israel. The Lord tells Moses to bless the people by saying,

> The LORD bless you
> 　　and keep you;
> the LORD make his face shine on you
> 　　and be gracious to you;
> the LORD turn his face toward you
> 　　and give you peace.

In this powerful blessing, peace has a much deeper meaning than calling for an end to physical violence and war. It does not mean to usher in a permanent state of tranquility. Here, the Lord's promise of peace is to make you whole.

As Black men, we are frequently encircled by multiform traumas. As a result, we have the lowest life expectancy of anyone in the nation. While we certainly long for an end to violence in our communities and for tranquility in our minds, our deeper longing, at times, is to be made whole, complete, restored, even favored. Much of the suffering we experience manifests from a sense of being incomplete, broken, unwell, and underappreciated.

Black man, listen to the blessing that the Lord speaks over your life. The Lord will bless you, keep you, place glory upon you, treat you well, and make you whole. Thankfully, no matter what we face, we do not face it alone. The Lord is with us, and we can be with and for each other too!

When the Lord gives us peace, we can say "Peace out!" to the drama from our traumas and walk in wholeness before the Lord.

Michael W. Waters

What are some areas where you desire to experience peace? List them, and speak God's blessing of Numbers 6:24–26 over yourself and those issues.

John 14:25–27

All this I have spoken while still with you. But the Advocate, the Holy Spirit, whom the Father will send in my name, will teach you all things and will remind you of everything I have said to you. Peace I leave with you; my peace I give you. I do not give to you as the world gives. Do not let your hearts be troubled and do not be afraid.

Conclusion

One of the teachers of the law came and heard
them debating. Noticing that Jesus had given
them a good answer, he asked him, "Of all the
commandments, which is the most important?"

Mark 12:28

There are a lot of debates out there about what makes a
"high-value man." The influencers who lead those debates
offer their rules for men that usually center on financial,
professional, and personal attributes and achievements that
are supposed to save us from being "low-value men." But
this isn't new.

We see in Mark 12:28 that men have been debating about
the rules for successful living since Bible times. But the life
of the brother in Mark 12 changed because he noticed "that
Jesus had given them a good answer," so he asked Him, "Of
all the commandments, which is the most important?" He
was a "teacher of the law," which meant he had his degree
and expertise, but he recognized that Jesus was different.

Unlike all the others in their debates, Jesus wasn't just
recycling someone else's opinion because he had a lot of
followers (although Jesus has more followers than anyone
in the history of TikTok, IG, or anywhere else). The teacher

of the law wanted to hear from Jesus, "How do I become a whole man?"

Jesus's response is the foundation of The Whole Man: "Love the Lord your God with all *your heart* and with all *your soul* and with all *your mind* and with all *your strength*" (Mark 12:30, emphasis added).

It is with our heart that we love God and others. As we have read in these reflections, we must reject the tendency as men to isolate ourselves and try to be our own like the Hollywood version of the "Lone Ranger." That version is a distortion. First of all, the real Lone Ranger, Bass Reeves, was Black. Additionally, the reality is that Reeves had help, and we need it as well. When we love God with all our hearts, we place our affections on Him above anything else.

It is with our soul that we bring our struggles to God. Our soul is the seat of our desires and decisions. Will we give in to our temptations or yield to the Holy Spirit within? Will we confess our shortcomings, or will we hide from God and from others? When we embrace the struggle within ourselves and turn it over to God, we experience a peace that passes all understanding.

It is with our minds and head that we pursue right thinking about God and ourselves. This includes the mental-health journey of confronting the lies that our traumatic experiences and those in our past told us. Black men often experience a stigma around getting therapy and counseling, but we must embrace the wisdom of Scripture: "Where no counsel is, the people fall: but in the multitude of counsellors there is safety" (Proverbs 11:14 KJV; see also Proverbs 18:4). If you are in need of a resource, check out wholebrothermission.com.

Lastly, it is with the strength of our hands that we do the work that God has called us to do. Work, though it can be frustrating and feel unrewarding, is a gift from God meant to make us more like Him. When we embrace our vocation—not just as a means to sustain ourselves or get rich or die trying, but as a means to participate in the kingdom of God—we find greater purpose and meaning. This also means resting. Sabbath is a key part of what we need to do with our hands. When we love God with all our strength, we're even willing to serve not based on trying to add to our net worth but out of our already-established kingdom worth.

This is what it means to be a whole man.

But this book is just the beginning. Make sure you continue the principles here in the following ways:

Create or join a small group. We have created video resources to help you build fellowship with other men on this journey. Go to experiencevoices.org /wholeman to get started. We also have group discussion questions ready for you.

Share The Whole Man *resources.* If you have been encouraged by your experience with *The Whole Man*, please share it with those around you. Encourage those in your circle to buy the book. Use #wholemanlife and post about the book, videos, and online resources. Buy a book for a brother who needs it. Sharing is caring!

Reach out to the Whole Brother Mission. Schedule a session with a Christian counselor or coach at wholebrothermission.com.

Take action. The Whole Man has four categories: head, heart, hands, soul. Pick an action step for each category to work on for the next forty days. Here are some examples:

- Head: Assess what is something you can do to improve your mental health.
- Heart: Take the next step in building a brotherhood with someone in your life.
- Hands: Identify a task to start doing or to take a Sabbath from doing.
- Soul: Find a practice you can engage in to help your soul be in touch with God's Spirit.

Holla back. Let us know what you think about *The Whole Man*. Give us a rating and a review wherever you get *The Whole Man* content. Also, you can give us a shout-out at experiencevoices.org/wholeman.

Blessings, brother. Thank you for allowing us to play a part in your journey to being a whole man.

Grace and peace,

Rasool Berry, Dr. Maliek Blade, Jerome Gay Jr.
General Editors

Acknowledgments

It takes a village to publish a book. Especially a book like this, which consists of multiple writers, editors, marketing teams, and supporters too many to name. We want to highlight just some who made *The Whole Man* possible.

I thank the Lord for granting enduring wisdom that enables us to look back and draw insights for life. I thank Chriscynethia for entrusting me with this project from the start, and Joyce, Katara, VOICES, and the entire Our Daily Bread Ministries team for the continued support. I also thank Tamica for being a life partner who has contributed so much to my journey of being a whole man.

—Rasool

Thank you, family and friends from the Whole Brother Mission who contributed and gave insight for both the video and written mediums for this project. Additionally, I'd like to thank my current and former clients: you have sharpened me by trusting me with your stories. Your stories have made my contributions to this project more well-rounded, compassionate, and insightful.

—Dr. Maliek

I thank Yeshua for His grace and mercy; my wife, Crystal, for her love, support, and wisdom; my children for being my motivation and inspiration; my family for always being in my corner; and the Vision Church family for allowing me to serve as your pastor. Lastly, I thank Our Daily Bread Ministries, Rasool, and Dr. Maliek for allowing me to be a part of this monumental project.

—Jerome

Notes

1. Pablo S. Torre, "How (and Why) Athletes Go Broke," *Sports Illustrated*, March 23, 2009, https://vault.si.com/vault/2009/03/23/how-and-why-athletes-go-broke.

2. Daniel A. Cox, "Men's Social Circles Are Shrinking," Survey Center on American Life, June 29, 2021, https://www.americansurveycenter.org/why-mens-social-circles-are-shrinking/.

3. Gregory James Tate, "The Decline in Black Men's Church Attendance: The Role of Male Presence in Church and the Family" (DMin diss., George Fox University, 2023), 1, https://digitalcommons.georgefox.edu/dmin/560/.

4. Anthony Hill, "Suicide Rate among Black Men and Boys on the Rise," ABC Action News, June 16, 2023, https://www.abcactionnews.com/news/in-depth/suicide-rate-among-black-men-and-boys-on-the-rise.

5. Lamin Sanneh, "Translation and the Incarnate Word: Scripture and the Frontier of Languages," in *Communicating the Word: Revelation, Translation, and Interpretation in Christianity and Islam*, ed. David Marshall (Washington, DC: Georgetown University Press, 2011), 72.

6. Philip Jenkins, *The New Faces of Christianity: Believing the Bible in the Global South* (Oxford: Oxford University Press, 2008), 9.

7. W. E. B. Du Bois, *The Souls of Black Folk: Essays and Sketches* (Chicago: A. C. McClurg & Co., 1903), 3.

8. Thong Teck Yew, "Kobe Bean Bryant: A Legend Never Forgotten," Medium, June 22, 2020, https://medium.com /illumination/kobe-bean-bryant-422b2cd573ff.

9. Joe Pantorno, "Oscar Robertson Comments on Stephen Curry, Modern NBA Game," Bleacher Report, February 25, 2016, https://bleacherreport.com/articles/2619777 -oscar-robertson-comments-on-stephen-curry-modern-nba -game.

10. Frederick Douglass, "The Church and Prejudice," University of Rochester Frederick Douglass Project, accessed March 19, 2024, https://rbscp.lib.rochester .edu/4369.

11. James Baldwin, "Black English: A Dishonest Argument," in *The Cross of Redemption: Uncollected Writings*, ed. Randall Kenan (New York: Vintage Books, 2010), 154.

12. Ethan Skolnick, "LeBron James Draws Inspiration from Bruce Lee, Mahatma Gandhi," Bleacher Report, January 3, 2014, https://bleacherreport.com/articles/1910030 -lebron-james-draws-inspiration-from-bruce-lee-also-a -huge-wrestling-guy.

13. Brett McCracken, "Keeping the Faith," *Christianity Today*, January 13, 2010, https://www.christianitytoday .com/ct/2010/januaryweb-only/denzelwashington-jan10 .html.

14. Philip Yancey, *Reaching for the Invisible God: What Can We Expect to Find?* (Grand Rapids, MI: Zondervan, 2000), 69.

About the General Editors

Rasool Berry is ministry partnership liaison and content developer with Our Daily Bread Ministries, the host of the *Where Ya From?* podcast, and the writer, producer, and host of the feature-length documentary *Juneteenth: Faith & Freedom*. He serves as the teaching pastor at Bridge Church in Brooklyn, New York. He graduated from the University of Pennsylvania with a degree in Africana studies and sociology. You can find his writings, podcasts, and videos at rasoolberry.com.

Facebook: Rasool Berry
Instagram: @rasoolb
X: @rasoolberry

Dr. Maliek Blade, a compassionate author and CEO of the Whole Brother Mission, is passionately dedicated to improving mental wellness for Black men and their families through a nationwide network of culturally competent mental-health professionals. With a doctoral-level background in counseling, he brings expertise and empathy to the cause, driving initiatives that destigmatize mental health and enhance access to crucial support. Dr. Maliek is the author of *Whole Brother: Debunking the Myths That Break the Black Family*, which you can find at maliekblade.com.

X: @maliekblade
Instagram: @maliekblade @wholebrothermission
TikTok: @wholebrothermission
Threads: @maliekblade @wholebrothermission

Jerome Gay Jr. is a native of Washington, DC, and serves as the lead pastor of teaching and vision at Vision Church. Jerome has a vision to see gospel-centered churches and leaders raised up within the urban context and sent out to plant other gospel-centered churches. He has his master's degree in Christian studies and ethics from Southeastern Baptist Theological Seminary. He is the author of several books including *The Whitewashing of Christianity*, which you can find on his website: jeromegayjr.com.

Instagram: @jeromegay
Threads: @jeromegay
Facebook: Pastor Jerome Gay Jr.
TikTok: @jeromegayjr2
X: @jeromegay
YouTube: youtube.com/theurbanperspective

Permissions

Scripture quotations, unless otherwise indicated, are taken from the Holy Bible, New International Version®, NIV®. Copyright © 1973, 1978, 1984, 2011 by Biblica, Inc.™ Used by permission of Zondervan. All rights reserved worldwide. www.zondervan.com.

Scripture quotations marked csb are taken from the Christian Standard Bible®, Copyright © 2017 by Holman Bible Publishers. Used by permission. Christian Standard Bible® and CSB® are federally registered trademarks of Holman Bible Publishers.

Scripture quotations marked esv are taken from the ESV® Bible (The Holy Bible, English Standard Version®), copyright © 2001 by Crossway, a publishing ministry of Good News Publishers. Used by permission. All rights reserved.

Scripture quotations marked kjv are taken from the Authorized Version, or King James Version, of the Bible.

Scripture quotations marked nasb are taken from the New American Standard Bible®, copyright © 1960, 1971, 1977, 1995, 2020 by The Lockman Foundation. Used by permission. All rights reserved. lockman.org.

Scripture quotations marked nkjv are taken from the New King James Version®. Copyright © 1982 by Thomas Nelson. Used by permission. All rights reserved.

See Us.

Hear Us.

Experience VOICES.

VOICES amplifies the strengths, struggles, and courageous faith of Black image bearers of God.

Podcasts, blogs, books, films, and more . . .

Find out more at **experiencevoices.org**

Spread the Word
by Doing One Thing.

- Give a copy of this book as a gift.
- Share the QR code link via your social media.
- Write a review of this book on your blog, favorite bookseller's website, or at ODB.org/store.
- Recommend this book to your church, small group, or book club.

Connect with us. 🅕 🅞

Our Daily Bread Publishing
PO Box 3566, Grand Rapids, MI 49501, USA
Email: books@odb.org

Love God. Love Others.

with  **Our Daily Bread.**

Your gift changes lives.

Connect with us. 🅕 ⓞ

Our Daily Bread Publishing
PO Box 3566, Grand Rapids, MI 49501, USA
Email: books@odb.org